LANG
BOOK PUBLISHING

Children's
Torah

Activity Book 2

By Belinda McCallion

LANG
BOOK PUBLISHING

langbookpublishing.com

National Library of New Zealand Cataloguing-in-Publication Data
Lang Book Publishing 2017

Co-edited by J. M. Betham-Lang and Roger Lang
Cover design by Blair McLean

ISBN 978-0-9941422-6-9

Published in New Zealand
A catalogue record for this book is available from the National Library of New Zealand.
Kei te pātengi raraunga o Te Puna Mātauranga o Aotearoa te whakarārangi o tēnei pukapuka.

This book Belongs to:

_____

How to use this book:

These worksheets have been especially designed for easy photocopy duplication.

Each lesson has 3 parts; a Torah, a Haftara and a B'rit Hadashah.

The main page of each part is the instruction page. This is not intended to replace the actual reading of the portion but to be a tool that can be used to summarise the readings and find a few key messages from the readings.

The activity page relates to the lesson and is intended to be used to reinforce the messages. This page caters to a wide age group, as there is always a picture to colour and a more difficult activity. Each activity sheet ranges in difficulty level dependant on the lesson. There is an answer page at the back of the book if you get stuck.

Table of Contents

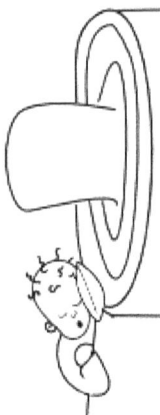

Parasha 13

Shemot

שמות שמות (Names) Exodus 1:1-6:1

Memory Verse

"G-d said further to Moshe, "Say this to the people of Isra'el: 'Yud-Heh-Vav-Heh [ADONAI], the G-d of your fathers, the G-d of Avraham, the G-d of Yitz'chak and the G-d of Ya'akov, has sent me to you.' This is my name forever; this is how I am to be remembered generation after generation."

Exodus 3:15CJB

Did You Know?

Shepherds are a symbol of ADONAI's leaders throughout the Bible. Moshe had to learn to be a shepherd in Midian.

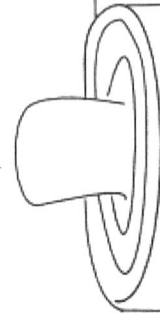

STORY SUMMARY

Story of Moshe: The generations of Isra'el are listed, including Moshe (Moses). Isra'el has grown large in the land, and a new pharaoh is now in charge. In fear that Isra'el might turn against Egypt, Pharaoh has them oppressed and made slaves. When this doesn't reduce their number, Pharaoh has the baby boys killed. Moshe is born and his parents hide him as long as they can before putting him in a basket in the river. Pharaoh's daughter finds him and raises him as her own. One day he kills an Egyptian for beating a Hebrew. Moshe flees into the desert. Here Moshe meets his wife and has an encounter with ADONAI in a burning bush. ADONAI commands him to go and tell Pharaoh to set His people free. With the help of Aaron, his brother, Moshe goes. ADONAI enables him to do miracles to convince the people that he is truly sent by ADONAI.

WORD FOCUS

Reuel: 'Friend of El.' This was the name of Moshe's father-in-law. Moshe's wife, Tzipporah, (Zipporah) was a descendant of Abraham through Keturah.

MAIN MESSAGE

ADONAI had a plan to save His people; He always has, and always will have. The Bible tells of this plan all the way through. Moshe doubted his own ability to carry out ADONAI's plan. He had to learn to obey, ADONAI would do the rest. We still struggle with this today. We think we can't do big things. All we need to do is obey and ADONAI will do the rest. Also, ADONAI will sometimes send us a sign to affirm His will.

TRUST   OBEY   SIGNS

Promise

Exodus 4:17 CJB

"And I have said that I will lead you up out of the misery of Egypt to the land of the Kena'ani, Hitti, Emori, P'rizi, Hivi and Y'vusi, to a land flowing with milk and honey."

Shemot Exodus 1:1-6:1 Activity Sheet

Baby Moshe

"When she could no longer hide him, she took a papyrus basket, coated it with clay and tar, put the child in it and placed it among the reeds on the riverbank. His sister stood at a distance to see what would happen to him."

Exodus 2:3-4 CJB

The Great Shepherd

ADONAI is the great shepherd who leads and guides His people. Help this shepherd lead his sheep through this maze.

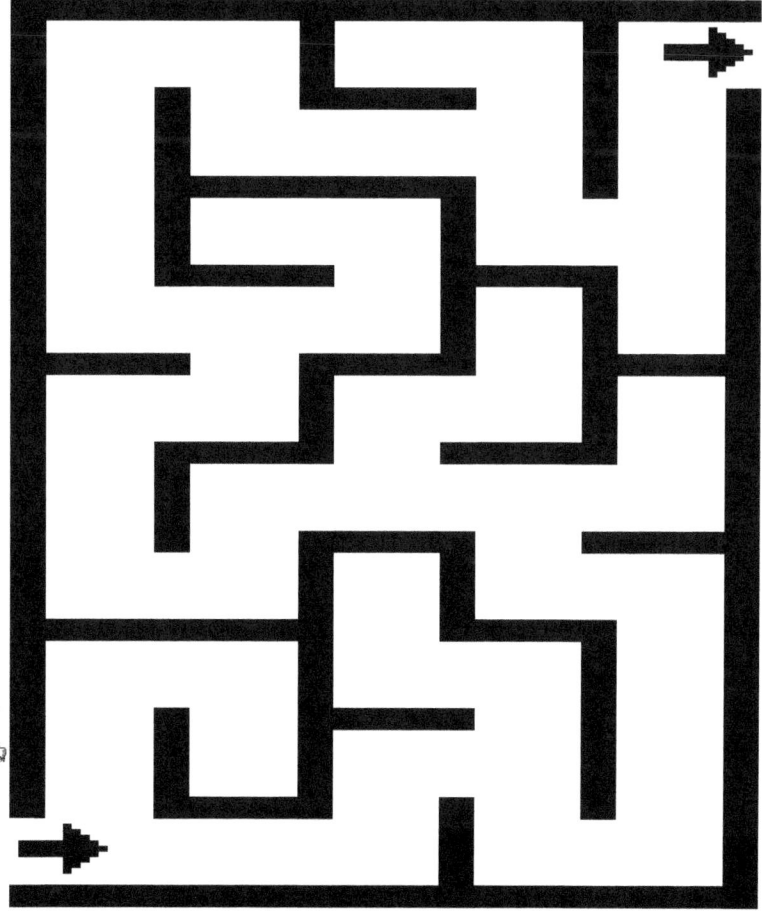

Yeshayahu

Isaiah 27:6-28:13

Promise

Isaiah 27:13 CJB

"On that day a great *shofar* will sound.

Those lost in the land of Ashur will come, also those scattered through the land of Egypt; and they will worship *ADONAI* on the holy mountain in Yerushalayim."

STORY SUMMARY

Prophecy of Isra'el's Future: Through Yeshayahu (Isaiah), ADONAI promises to once again show Isra'el favour– her exile has been served and she will be bought back. Her enemies will be humbled. Despite her unclean state she will be cleansed and made acceptable. Until then, she will be taught like a child; precept by precept, line by line, a little here and a little there.

WORD FOCUS

Tzav: 'Command' This word has often been translated as precept. Isra'el will be taught like a child– command by command.

MAIN MESSAGE

Many of the children of Isra'el had blended in with the Egyptians and had learned their ways. When ADONAI sent the plagues that only affected the Egyptians, this was a message to both the Egyptians and the Hebrews that ADONAI knew who His people were and desired them to be different. After all this time we still do not fully understand, so we still need to be taught the basic truths. ADONAI still knows who His people are and He still wants us to be different from the world. He is active in the world today, changing lives and preparing His people for His return.

SET-APART   CHOSEN   FAITHFUL

Haftara 13 (Prophets)

Memory Verse

"The time is coming when Ya'akov will take root; Isra'el will bud and flower, and fill the whole world with a harvest."

Isaiah 27:6 CJB

Did You Know?

Isra'el would become a light to the nations by being scattered into the nations.

Yeshayahu (Isaiah 27:6-28:13) Activity Sheet

A Glorious Crown

"On that day, ADONAI-Tzva'ot will be a glorious crown, a brilliant diadem for the remnant of His people."

Isaiah 28:5 CJB

Tzav La Tzav

Isaiah 28:10 records a nursery rhyme used to teach the things of ADONAI. Join up the right connections to see the Hebrew and English translation together.

Line by line

A little here/there

Precept by precept

Tzav la-tzav

Kav la-kav

Z'eir sham

Matthew
2:13 -19
B'rit Hadashah 13
(Newer Testament)

STORY SUMMARY

Fleeing to Egypt: An angel tells Yosef (Joseph) in a dream to take Miryam (Mary) and Yeshua, and flee to Egypt until Herod is no longer a threat. This is to fulfil the prophesy given in Isaiah 40:3. Likewise, the sorrow of Rachel described in Jeremiah 31:14(15)* is fulfilled in Herod's order to kill the baby boys.

WORD FOCUS

Male, Mala, Maley: 'to full, to fill.' When something is fulfilled, it is more complete; not done away with.

MEMORY VERSE

"After they had gone, an angel of *ADONAI* appeared to Yosef in a dream and said, 'Get up, take the child and his mother, and escape to Egypt, and stay there until I tell you to leave...'" Matthew 2:13 CJB

MAIN MESSAGE

Many prophecies in the Bible have more than one fulfilment. Just as ADONAI called Isra'el His children and bought them out of Egypt, so He called His son, Yeshua, out of Egypt. ADONAI is now calling his children out of sin, which is also symbolised as Egypt.

PROMISE

"Out of Egypt I will call my son." Isaiah 40:3 CJB

DID YOU KNOW?

Hebrew thinking is in cycles rather than in timelines. These double-meaning prophecies are examples of this cycle style of thinking.

* verse 15 in other translations

Matthew 2:13-19 Activity Sheet

Fleeing to Egypt

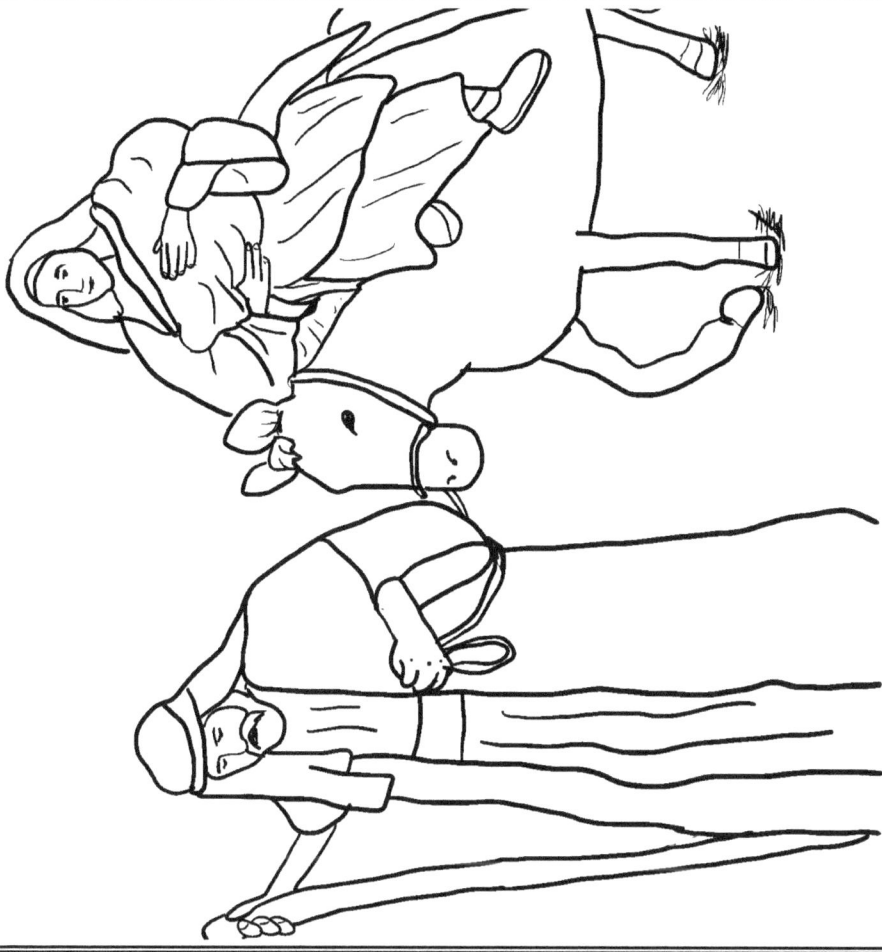

"So he got up, took the child and his mother, and left during the night for Egypt." Matthew 2:14 CJB

Following Directions

Yosef listened to what ADONAI said. Here is another maze. This time, follow these directions to make it through.

Go right, down, left, down, left, down, right, 2nd up, right down, right, up, right, down, left, down, right, up, right, up, left, down, left, up, right, down, left, up, left, down, 3rd right, up, right ,up, right ,down, left, down, right, down, right, and down.

Parasha 14

פרשה ואראָ **Vaera** (I appeared) Exodus 6:2-9:35

Memory Verse

"I appeared to Avraham, Yitz'chak and Ya'akov as *El Shaddai*, although I did not make myself known to them by my name, *Yud-Heh-Vav-Heh* [*ADONAI*]."

Exodus 6:3 CJB

Did You Know?

Moshe was eighty years old when he went to Pharaoh.

Promise

Exodus 6:6 CJB

"Therefore, say to the people of Isra'el: 'I am *ADONAI*. I will free you from the forced labor of the Egyptians, rescue you from their oppression, and redeem you with an outstretched arm and with great judgments.'"

STORY SUMMARY

ADONAI Sends Plagues: The people of Isra'el do not believe Moshe's words of deliverance from ADONAI. Neither does Pharaoh listen to him. The sign of the rod turning into a snake can be copied by the magicians, even though Moshe's snake swallows up their snakes. ADONAI sends more signs in the form of plagues. First the river turns to blood, next frogs invade the land, then lice, followed by wild beasts. After that the livestock of the Egyptians are struck down (not the Hebrew's), then infectious sores. Next a great hail storm comes. Throughout all of this, Pharaoh makes promises to let the Hebrews go and worship if ADONAI stops the plagues, but Pharaoh goes against his word and remains hard, just as ADONAI said he would.

WORD FOCUS

Arov: 'A mixture.' This word was used to describe the fourth plague. It is understood as a mixture of wild beasts. Some translations use 'insects or flies' because they understand the word to mean 'a swarm'. Most Jewish sources agree that this plague was 'wild beasts.'

MAIN MESSAGE

ADONAI establishes His name. He also reveals His ability and desire to save whole nations, not just individuals. The plagues come in three sets, and all follow a similar pattern. Apart from the outcome of setting Isra'el free, there is another purpose to the plagues. The first three are to prove that ADONAI is G-d. The next three show that ADONAI is present in the land and in the lives of His people, and the last three show that ADONAI is unique and like no other. Next week's parasha deals with the final plagues.

ONE TRUE G-D   FAITHFULNESS   POWER

Vaera Exodus 6:2-9:35 Activity Sheet

The Plague of Frogs

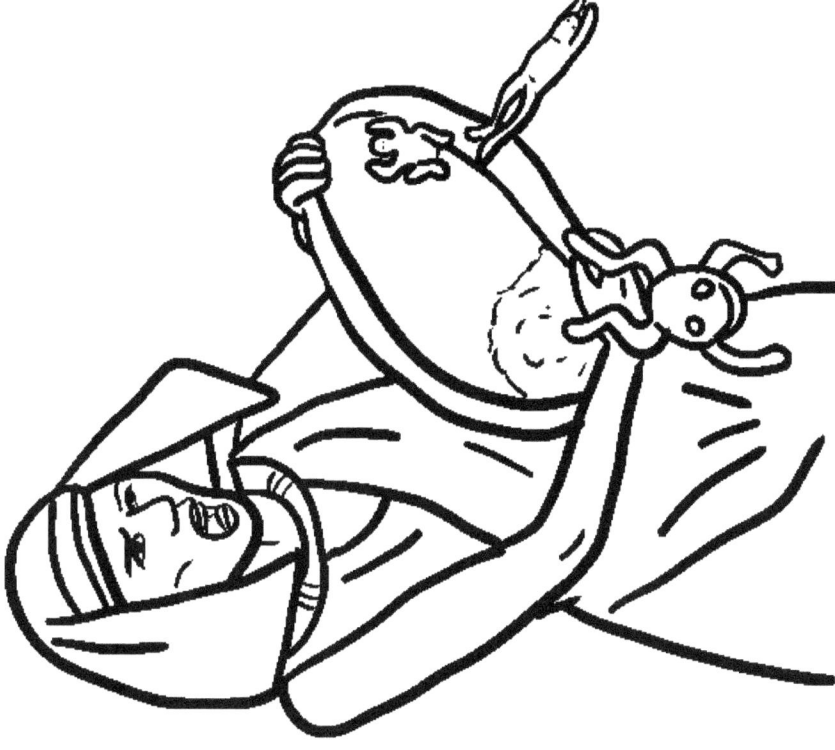

"The river will swarm with frogs. They will go up, enter your palace and go into your bedroom, onto your bed. They will enter the houses of your servants and your people and go into your ovens and kneading bowls."

Exodus 7:28 (8:2)* CJB   *in other translations

The Plagues

Seven of the ten plagues are talked about in this parasha. Write what they are next to the pictures.

Yechezk'el (Ezekiel) 28:25-29:21

Promise

Ezekiel 28:25 CJB

"*ADONAI ELOHIM* says, 'Once I have gathered the house of Isra'el from the peoples among whom they are scattered, once I have shown my holiness in them as the *Goyim* watch, then they will live in their own land, which I gave to my servant Ya'akov.'"

STORY SUMMARY

Pharaoh's Downfall: Yechezk'el delivers a message from ADONAI, first to Isra'el and then to Egypt. He tells Isra'el that He will bring them back into their land, they will live in safety and ADONAI will take care of their hateful neighbours. To Pharaoh in Egypt, ADONAI predicts forty years of exile and destruction. This is because Pharaoh boasts in his own abilities to create the Nile river.

WORD FOCUS

Nava (Naba): 'To prophesy.' This means, to predict something that will happen in the future by divine inspiration.

MAIN MESSAGE

All the different Pharaohs viewed themselves as gods. Through humbling them, HaShem showed that He alone is the sustainer of life and the only true G-d. Likewise many today believe themselves to be the creators of their own achievements and do not acknowledge ADONAI as the source. We should always remember to give ADONAI the credit He alone is due.

HUMILITY   CONSEQUENCES   JUSTICE

Haftara 14 (Prophets)

Memory Verse

"...I will reduce them, so that they never again rule other nations."

Ezekiel 29:15 CJB

Did You Know?

Cleopatra was the last Pharaoh. She died in 30 BCE.

Yechezk'el (Ezekiel 28:25-29:21) Activity Sheet

Pharaoh

Black out every second line, then write out the remaining letters on the blanks to reveal what ADONAI wanted Pharaoh and Egypt to know.

Three of them have been done for you.

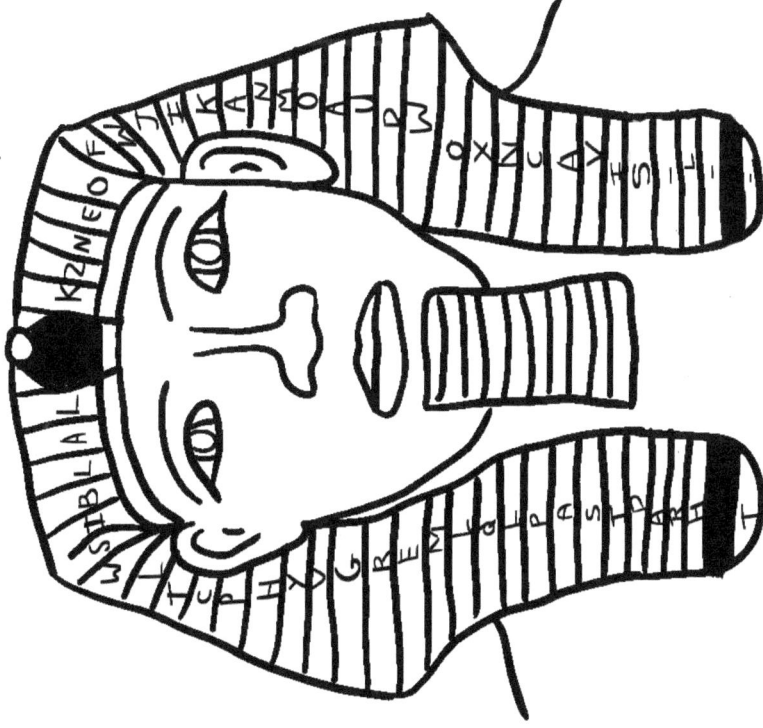

___ ___ ___ ___ ___ ___ ___ ___ ___

___ ___ ___ ___ ___ ___ ___ ___ ___

___ ___ ___ ___ ___ ___

Pharaoh the Crocodile

"...I am against you, Pharaoh king of Egypt, you big crocodile lying in the streams of the Nile! You say, 'My Nile is mine; I made it for myself.'"   Ezekiel 29:3 CJB

Luke 22:14-20

B'rit Hadashah 14
(Newer Testament)

STORY SUMMARY

Passover Seder: Before Yeshua dies, He has a seder with His disciples. During the ceremony, Yeshua reveals the meaning of the cups of the 'fruit of the vine,' and the breaking of unleavened bread. Yeshua says, "do this in memory of me," because He will not have another seder until the kingdom comes. At this time the full meaning will be revealed.

WORD FOCUS

Seder: 'Order or arrangement.' It is a ritual feast that marks the beginning of Passover.

MEMORY VERSE

"...do this in memory of me." Luke 22:19 CJB

MAIN MESSAGE

The four cups of the Passover seder represent the deliverance from Egypt. These four cups show it is ADONAI who will; bring you, deliver you, redeem you and take you. We are still waiting for the completion of this. While we wait, we are to symbolically remember Yeshua through this seder.

PROMISE

"For I tell you, it is certain that I will not celebrate it again until it is given its full meaning in the Kingdom of G-d." Luke 22:16 CJB

DID YOU KNOW?

The cup talked about here is the fourth cup of the seder.

"When the time came, Yeshua and the emissaries reclined at the table, and He said to them, 'I have really wanted so much to celebrate this *Seder* with you before I die!'"

Luke 22:14-15 CJB

Through all the symbols in the festivals, ADONAI wants us to 'remember.' The way we remember something is to repeat it often. A memory verse is a verse we can remember without looking it up. Memorise the memory verse. If you are want more of a challenge, memorise the full verse.

"Also, taking a piece of *matzah*, he made the *b'rakhah* (blessing), broke it, gave it to them and said, 'This is my body, which is being given for you; **do this in memory of me.'"** Luke 22:19 CJB

Parasha 15

פרשה בא

(Go) Exodus 10:1-13:16

Bo

Promise

Exodus 13:9 CJB

"This was a night when ADONAI kept vigil to bring them out of the land of Egypt, and this same night continues to be a night when ADONAI keeps vigil for all the people of Isra'el through all their generations."

Memory Verse

"...With a strong hand ADONAI brought us out of Egypt, out of the abode of slavery."

Exodus 13:14 CJB

Did You Know?

Being free does not mean we are now our own boss. It means we have changed ownership. ADONAI is now our master instead of sin.

STORY SUMMARY

ADONAI Delivers His People: Egypt has just seen seven of the ten plagues. Now the last three plagues are about to come. First comes locusts, then darkness. This will be followed by the death of the firstborn males. ADONAI, through Moshe, instructs His people to take a lamb, use the blood to cover the door posts of their houses, then eat the meat in their homes with their families. By doing this, when the plague of death comes, it will not come upon them or their families. After this plague, Pharaoh lets the Isra'elites go. They leave in a hurry and eat bread that has not had time to rise. ADONAI, through Moshe, tells the people how to remember this time every year, generation after generation. It is known as Pesach or Passover.

WORD FOCUS

Abad: 'Slavery', 'servant' or 'bondage.' To be a slave to sin means you are under sin's control. ADONAI frees us from this bondage of sin so that we can live with victory over sin.

MAIN MESSAGE

We are redeemed by ADONAI through the blood of the Lamb. Yeshua became this lamb for us. Through His blood we are delivered from the Egypt of sin. One day we will again be physically redeemed into His kingdom. Meanwhile, there is a spiritual redemption from the sin that surrounds us. By claiming the blood of the lamb, we are giving ADONAI authority in our lives, to deliver us from sin and make us clean. Pesach is a time of year to really focus on these things.

DELIVERANCE   REDEMPTION   FAITH

Bo Exodus 10:1-13:16 Activity Sheet

Blood on the Doorpost

"They are to take some of the blood and smear it on the two sides and top of the door-frame at the entrance of the house in which they eat it." Exodus 12:7 CJB

The Firstborn

If you were in Egypt at the time of Pesach, who in your family would have been saved by the blood on the doorpost? List the firstborn men in your family that you know. You can include relatives such as your immediate family, grandparents, uncles, cousins and

so on.

Yirmeyahu

(Jeremiah) 46:13-28

Haftara 15 (Prophets)

Memory Verse

"Yet don't be afraid, Ya'akov my servant; don't be distressed, Isra'el..."

Jeremiah 46:27 CJB

Did You Know?

Locusts are kosher to eat.

Promise

Jeremiah 46:27 CJB

"...For I will save you from faraway places, and your offspring from the lands where they are held captive. Ya'akov will return and be at peace, quiet, with no one to make him afraid."

STORY SUMMARY

Egypt's Destruction: ADONAI, through Yirmeyahu, predicts how Egypt will be invaded by N'vukhadretzar (Nebuchadnezzar) of Bavel (Babylon). This is because of Egypt's false worship and cruel treatment of Isra'el.

WORD FOCUS

Bavel: 'Babylon' also 'to jumble.' This comes from the word 'balal.' Bavel is also known to mean 'the gate of G-d.'

MAIN MESSAGE

The locust plague of Egypt was greater than ever. However, the invasion from Babylon would be greater. Many times people do not learn from past mistakes in history and have to experience the consequences again. Egypt did not learn that Isra'el was special to ADONAI, and He would defend them. Unfortunately, they needed to be shown again. It is wise to take advice from people who can help save us from making bad choices. It is good to learn from history and the mistakes of others. This can save a lot of unnecessary pain.

PRIDE   CONSEQUENCES   LISTENING

Note: Parental discretion advised when using biblical narrative

Yirmeyahu (Jeremiah 46:13-28) Activity Sheet

King N'vukhadretzar

"This word ADONAI spoke to Yirmeyahu the prophet concerning how N'vukhadretzar king of Bavel would come and attack the land of Egypt." Jeremiah 46:13 CJB

Destruction

While destruction was being spoken over Egypt, ADONAI had a special comforting message for Isra'el. Part of this message of Jeremiah 46:27 is written in this rubble. Rewrite it in the right order.

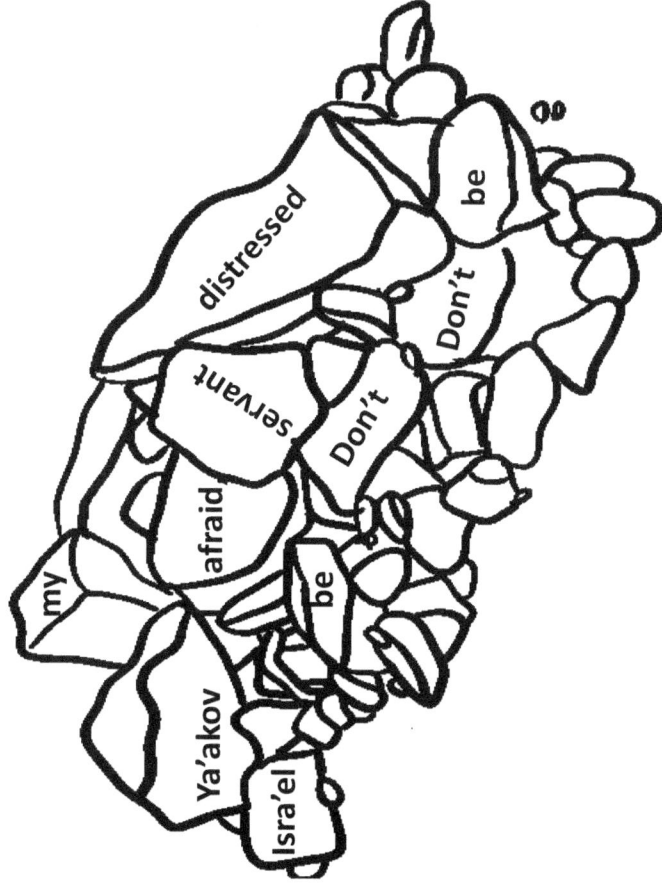

_____

_____

_____

1 Peter
1:18-21

B'rit Hadashah 15
(Newer Testament)

STORY SUMMARY

Yeshua the Pesach Lamb: The price paid to ransom us from a worthless life was not silver or gold, but something more precious. It was the blood sacrifice of Yeshua as the Lamb. ADONAI knew Him before time began and revealed Him as the Messiah, who died and was raised again. He gave ADONAI all glory and inspired people to put their trust and hope in ADONAI.

WORD FOCUS

Kopher: 'Ransom.' This has the same root word as 'atonement', which also sums up well what the blood of Yeshua does for us.

MEMORY VERSE

"...But with the precious blood of the Messiah, like that of a lamb without blemish or defect."
1 Peter 1:19 ISV

MAIN MESSAGE

The Pesach story of redemption highlights the plan of salvation by showing how ADONAI has been working to redeem His people. Understanding Yeshua's blood sacrifice as the Lamb improves our understanding of Pesach, and should lead us to appreciate this festival more, realising how much our freedom cost ADONAI.

PROMISE

"Through Him you trust in G-d, who raised Him from the dead and gave Him glory; so that your trust and hope are in G-d." 1 Peter 1:21 CJB

DID YOU KNOW?

ADONAI still wants us to remember Pesach and teach our children about it.

1 Peter 1:18-21 Activity Sheet

Inheritance

1 Peter 1:18 says we inherit a worthless life from our forefathers. When we choose Yeshua our lives are no longer worthless. Below, in various translations, are some other words used to describe the life we inherit from our forefathers. Unscramble them.

pemyt NIV

_____

lituef ESV

_____

nvia KJV

_____

lsusese WEB

_____

hofolsi YLT

_____

Freedom from Sin

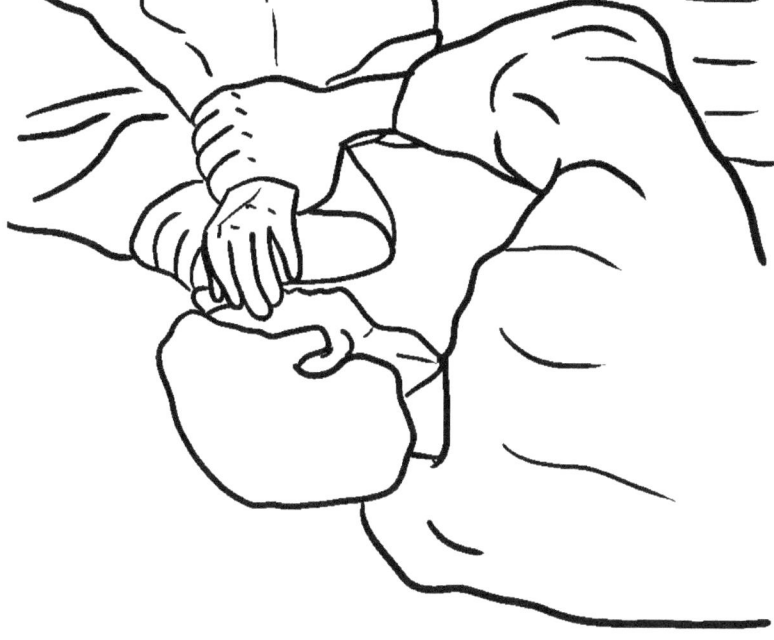

"You should be aware that the ransom paid to free you from the worthless way of life which your fathers passed on to you did not consist of anything perishable like silver or gold..." 1 Peter 1:18 CJB

Parasha 16

Memory Verse

"...Because their hand was against the throne of *Yah*, *ADONAI* will fight 'Amalek generation after generation."
Exodus 17:16 CJB

Did You Know?

The Red Sea is also known as the Sea of Reeds, or the Sea of Suf.

בשלח פרשת **Beshalach** (When He sent) Exodus 13:17-17:16

STORY SUMMARY

The Journey Begins: The Children of Isra'el have just been delivered from Egypt. Now ADONAI leads them towards the promised land. He doesn't take the highway, instead He leads them through the desert. Along the way, Isra'el are faced with obstacles, such as a big sea to cross, no water to drink and no food to eat. Through these experiences, ADONAI shows His power and guidance. He is also with them in the form of a pillar of cloud by day and fire by night. ADONAI performs miracles, such as parting the sea and destroying Pharaoh's army and providing water to drink and quail and manna to eat. Yet each time they face a new challenge, the people are fearful and they complain. The next obstacle they face is the military attack of Amalek. Yohoshua leads the battle, while Moshe, Aharon and Hur seek ADONAI. Moshe needs to keep his hands raised in order for Isra'el to win. Aharon and Hur hold his arms up until Amalek is defeated.

WORD FOCUS

Amalek: 'Dweller in a valley.' He was said to be Esau's grandson, but is also referred to at other times. This suggests there is a spiritual meaning to who he is. Hebrew tradition says Amalek represents pure evil, or those who have given themselves over to evil. ADONAI fights Amalek throughout all generations.

MAIN MESSAGE

Have you ever wondered why something has happened the way it did? We can't always understand why ADONAI leads in a certain way, but He always knows best. He led Isra'el in the exact course that they needed to survive and grow. From this lesson we can learn that instead of complaining when things go wrong for us, we can fully trust in ADONAI that He has our best interest at heart, even when we don't understand. We just need to be obedient and keep trusting that He will come through for us.

REMEMBER   TRUST   BE GRATEFUL

Promise

Exodus 14:13 CJB

"...Stop being so fearful! Remain steady, and you will see how *ADONAI* is going to save you. He will do it today — today you have seen the Egyptians, but you will never see them again!"

Mighty to Save

Exodus 14:8 said the people left boldly. ADONAI showed them, they did not leave in their own strength. Use this sign language code to reveal when the people realised ADONAI was with them. Be careful, some letters look very similar to others.

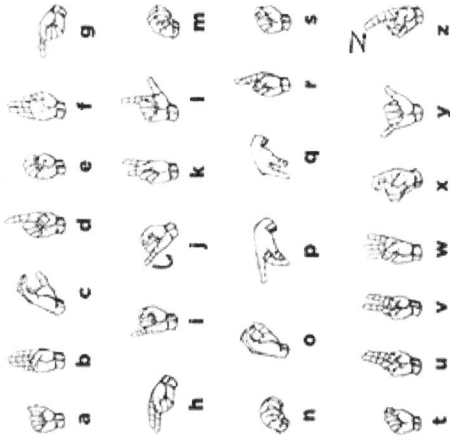

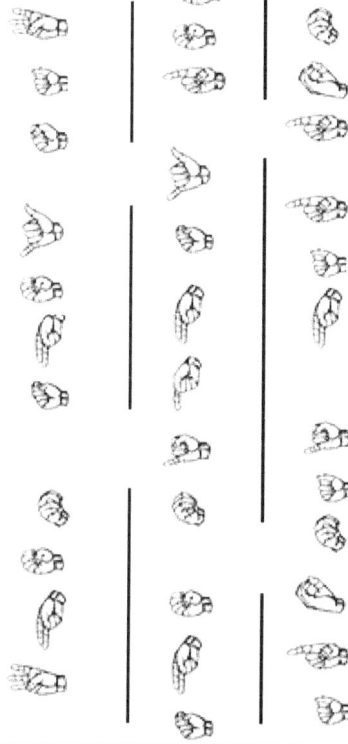

a b c d e f g

h i j k l m

n o p q r s

t u v w x y z

Battle Against Amalek

"When Moshe raised his hand, Isra'el prevailed; but when he let it down, 'Amalek prevailed. However, Moshe's hands grew heavy; so they took a stone and put it under him, and he sat on it. Aharon and Hur held up his hands, the one on the one side and the other on the other; so that his hands stayed steady until sunset."

Exodus 17:11-12 CJB

Shoftim

Haftara 16 (Prophets)

(Judges) 5:1-31

Memory Verse

"Hear, kings; listen, princes; I will sing to *ADONAI*! I will sing praise to *ADONAI* the G-d of Isra'el."

Judges 5:3 CJB

Did You Know?

Your heartbeat changes and mimics the music you are listening to.

STORY SUMMARY

Song of D'vorah: ADONAI, through D'vorah (Deborah), led Isra'el to be victorious over Caanan, who were ruling them harshly. She and Barak sang a song to praise ADONAI and record the story.

WORD FOCUS

D'vorah: 'Honey Bee.' Traditionally the Jews have compared themselves to bees in a number of ways. One example is that bees are servants. This is a reminder to stay humble like a bee.

MAIN MESSAGE

Similarly to the parasha, when Miriam sang a song after being delivered by ADONAI from Egypt, D'vorah sang a song after ADONAI worked through her to deliver Isra'el from Sisra of Caanan. Praising ADONAI in song is a great way to lift your mood and worship ADONAI. It is also a great way to remember scripture.

PRAISE   SING   HUMILITY

Promise

Judges 5:31 CJB

"May all your enemies perish like this, *ADONAI*; but may those who love Him be like the sun going forth in its glory!"

Note: Parental discretion advised when using biblical narrative

Shoftim (Judges 5:1-31) Activity Sheet

D'vorah Leads Isra'el

"Awake, awake, D'vorah! Awake, awake, awake, break into song! Arise, Barak! Lead away your captives, son of Avino'am!" Judges 5:12 CJB

Writing a Song

In English, songs usually rhyme. Can you write a rhyming song about something ADONAI has done for you? Sing it to the tune of another song you know. One Hint for getting good rhyming words is to write out the alphabet along the top of your paper and go through each letter to see which words might rhyme with the word at the end of your sentence. If you can't find a word, you might need to change the word you are trying to rhyme.

A B C D E F G H I J K L M N O P Q R S T U V W X Y Z

1 Thessalonians B'rit Hadashah 16
4:16-17   (Newer Testament)

STORY SUMMARY

The Resurrection: Yeshua will one day return and gather His people, starting with those who have already died, followed by those who are living.

WORD FOCUS

Yashir: 'will sing.' In the parasha this is written as 'to sing', but in Hebrew grammar, this word is a future tense word.

MEMORY VERSE

"For the Lord Himself will come down from heaven with a rousing cry, with a call from one of the ruling angels, and with G-d's *shofar*; those who died united with the Messiah will be the first to rise."

1 Thessalonians 4:16 CJB

MAIN MESSAGE

The sages believed the song of Miriam recorded in the parasha was a prophesy of the song that will be sung at the resurrection of the dead. At that time, all who have put their hope and trust in ADONAI will experience the promised eternal life. This does not happen when we die, but when we are resurrected.

PROMISE

"Then we who are left still alive will be caught up with them in the clouds to meet the Lord in the air; and thus we will always be with the Lord."

1 Thessalonians 4:17 CJB

DID YOU KNOW?

The Bible says dead people do not know anything.

1 Thessalonians 4:16-17 Activity Sheet

The Promise

Every generation of believers since Yeshua have been waiting for His Second Coming. Colour in the 'awake' eyes to reveal what this promise give us in our lives.

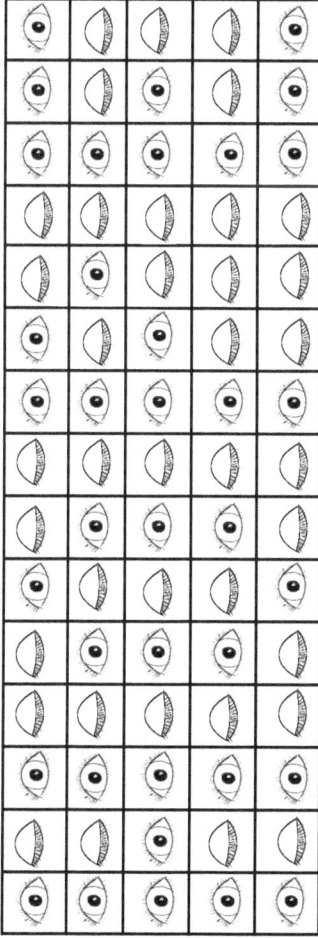

The Second Coming

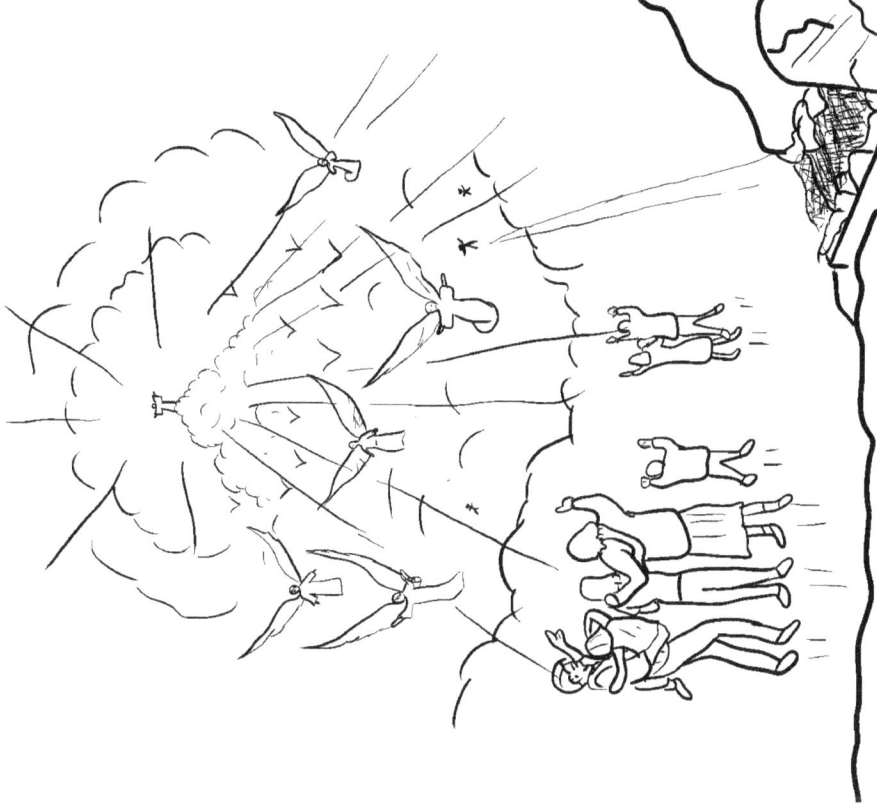

"Then we who are left still alive will be caught up with them in the clouds to meet the Lord in the air; and thus we will always be with the Lord." 1 Thessalonians 4:17 CJB

Parasha 17

Memory Verse

"You should also teach them the Laws and the Teachings, and show them how to live their lives and what work they should do."

Exodus 18:20 CJB

Did You Know?

There were over two million Isra'elites in the wilderness.

YITRO

יִתְרוֹ

(Jethro) Exodus 18:1-20:23

STORY SUMMARY

Moshe (Moses) Family Reunited: Moshe's father-in-law, Yitro, brings his wife and sons to him in the wilderness. While he is there, Yitro tells Moshe to choose leaders to help him serve the people and guide them.

ADONAI Comes Down: ADONAI makes a covenant with Isra'el. Moshe meets ADONAI on Mt. Sinai where ADONAI tells the people the law.

WORD FOCUS

Vehizharthah: 'To make the law of ADONAI shine brightly.' This shows how important the law is. When we obey ADONAI, we too shine brightly.

MAIN MESSAGE

The last part of the memory verse talks about knowing what work you should do. This shows how much ADONAI wants us to serve others and think of their needs before our own. Loving ADONAI and loving each other is the main focus of the law. ADONAI wants us to remember His law, and keep it in our heart, so it changes us. We also love by showing respect to elders and teachers.

LOVE   SERVE   REMEMBER   RESPECT

Promise

Exodus 19:5 CJB

"Now if you pay careful attention to what I say and keep my covenant, then you will be my own treasure from among all the people..."

YITRO Exodus 18:1-20:23 Activity Sheet

ADONAI told the Isra'elites 10 things He wanted them to obey. Help them to remember the order they were spoken. Draw a line from the number to the commandment.

1.
2. Do not desire your neighbours things
3. Honour your father and mother
4.
5.
6.
7. Don't commit adultery
8.
9.
10.

Remember the Shabbat (Sabbath) day to keep it holy

Have NO other Gods before me

Don't tell lies about people

Don't Murder

Don't steal

Don't use the Name of YHWH your G-d lightly

Don't make any carved images representing me or any living thing to worship. Worship only me.

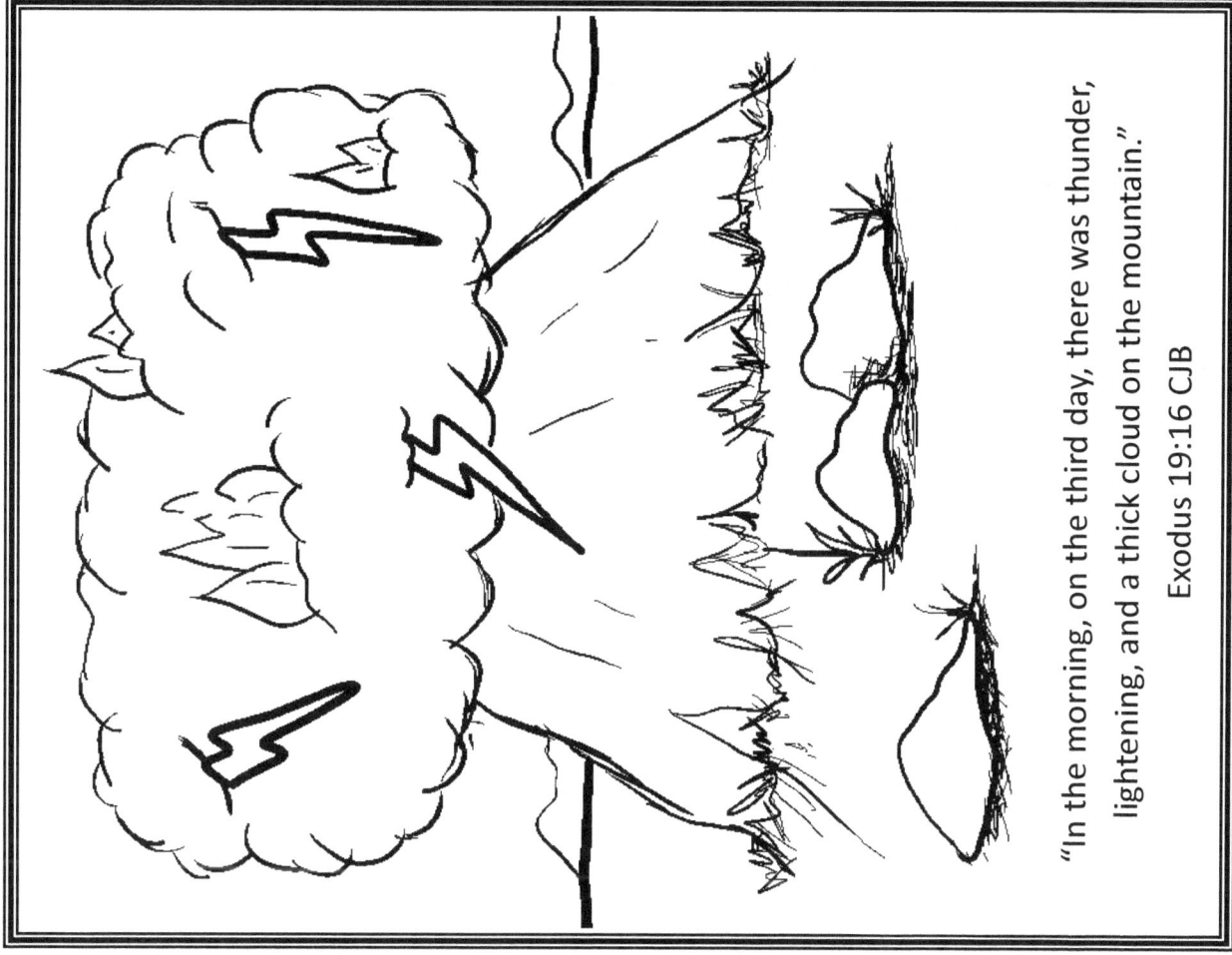

"In the morning, on the third day, there was thunder, lightening, and a thick cloud on the mountain."

Exodus 19:16 CJB

27

Yeshayahu

Isaiah 6:1-7:6; 9:5-6

Haftara 17 (Prophets)

Memory Verse

"'Whom should I send, and who will go for us?' I answered 'I'm here, send me!'"

Isaiah 6:8 CJB

Did You Know?

Isaiah was the most-quoted prophet in the New Testament (B'rit Hadashah)

STORY SUMMARY

Yeshayahu (Isaiah) Called by ADONAI to be His Voice to the People:

Yeshayahu sees a glorious vision of ADONAI on His throne. ADONAI cleanses Isaiah, who then says he is willing to be ADONAI's messenger. ADONAI tells Isaiah to call the people to repent and stop doing evil things. He also tells him of future battles and beyond. This is followed by a prophecy of the coming Messiah.

WORD FOCUS — Names of the Messiah

Pele-Yo'etz: Wonderful Counselor,   **El Gibbor:** Mighty G-d,

Avi-'Ad: Our Everlasting Father,   **Sar-Shalom:** Prince of Peace

MAIN MESSAGE

Yeshua is the baby who came as a son given for us. He is our Wonderful Counselor, Mighty G-d, Everlasting Father and Prince of Peace. ADONAI uses people to reach people. Will you be willing to be used if He calls you to tell people about Yeshua? All the titles listed here are all about Him.

OBEY   **SERVE**   **HONOUR**

Promise

Isaiah 9:5-6 CJB

"For a child is born to us, a son is given to us; dominion will rest on his shoulders, and he will be given the name '...Wonder of a counselor, mighty G-d, Father of Eternity, Prince of Peace, in order to extend the dominion and perpetuate the peace of the throne and kingdom of David to secure it and sustain it through justice and righteousness henceforth and forever. The Zeal of ADONAI will accomplish this."

28

Seraphim

"Seraphim stood over him, each with six wings– two for covering his face , two for covering his feet and two for flying". Isaiah 6:2 CJB

Names of ADONAI

Write the English names for the Hebrew names in the clues.

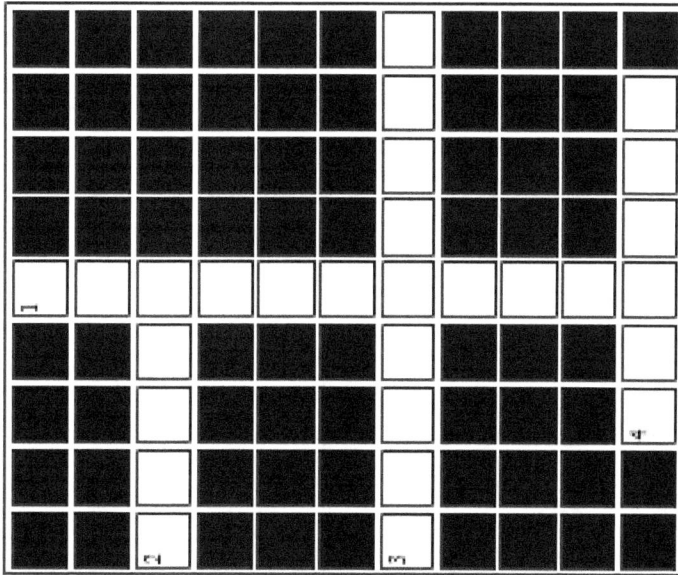

Across

2. Sar-Shalom : Prince of _____

3. Pele-Yo 'etz :Wonderful _____

4. El Gibbor : _____ G-d

Down

1. Avi-'Ad : Our _____ Father

1 Corinthians   B'rit Hadashah 17
12:7-13   (Newer Testament)

STORY SUMMARY

Gifts of the Spirit: As believers, we are members of the family of ADONAI. He gives us the spiritual gifts and wants us to use them to help others in the kehilah of Yeshua. These gifts are:
WISDOM, KNOWLEDGE, FAITH, HEALING, MIRACLES, PROPHECY, DISCERNMENT, TONGUES, INTERPRETATION OF TONGUES.

WORD FOCUS

Kahillah: Community. Yeshua wants us to be a true community with each other. He wants us to love and help each other through good times and bad times.

MEMORY VERSE

"The *Ruach HaKodesh* is given to each of us in a special way. That is for the good of all."
1 Cor 12:7 NIrV

MAIN MESSAGE

Loving and caring for each other is very important to ADONAI. For His kahillah to be healthy, this needs to be the most important thing after loving Him. We can't have this kind of love on our own. We need His Ruach (Spirit) living in us to teach us how to love others this way. You can ask ADONAI for the Ruach HaKodesh to help you.

PROMISE

"But when the Spirit of Truth comes, He will guide you into all truth." John 16:13 NIrV

DID YOU KNOW?

Shaul (Paul), like all Jewish Torah students, would have memorised the whole Torah.

1 Corinthians 12:7-13 Activity Sheet

Kahillah

"...The parts of the body will not take sides. All of them will take care of each other. If one part suffers, every part will suffer with it. If one part is honoured, every part will share in it's joy." 1 Corinthians 12: 25-26 NIrV

Gifts of the Ruach

Help the kahillah serve each other by matching the person with the gift to the person who needs it.

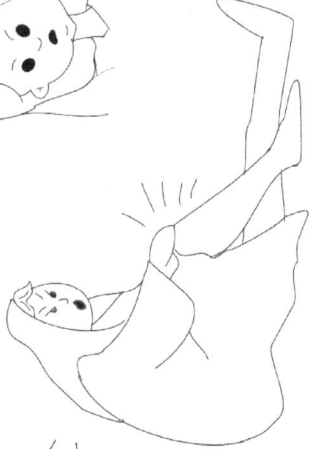

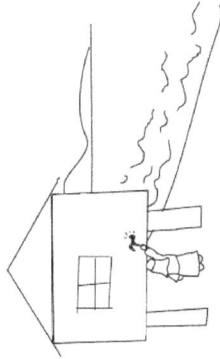

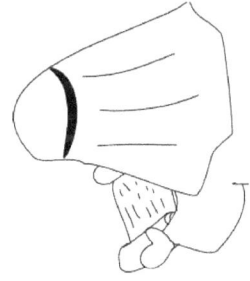
KNOWLEDGE

WISDOM

HEALING

Promise

Exodus 23:25 CJB

"You are to serve *ADONAI* your God; and He will bless your food and water. I will take sickness away from among you."

Mishpatim

מִשְׁפָּטִים (Rulings) Exodus 18:1-20:23

STORY SUMMARY

More of the Life Instructions are Given: ADONAI, through Moshe (Moses), continues to tell the people what they are to do in many different situations, and how He feels about certain behaviours such as murder and cruelty to others. The people agree to do what ADONAI has asked them to do and a covenant is made. Then Moshe goes up the mountain with Y'hohua into ADONAI's presence. The cloud of ADONAI's presence looked like a raging fire to the people below.

WORD FOCUS

Mishpatim: 'Rulings or judgements.' This comes from the root word 'to judge.' ADONAI is also described as a righteous judge. This shows the importance ADONAI places on justice.

MAIN MESSAGE

The Ten Commandments are not all ADONAI had to say on how to live. There were many other things that were told to the people to keep their community happy and healthy. The theme of these rulings was to love others and treat people justly. This is still relevant today.

LOVE   JUSTICE   RESPECT

Parasha 18

Memory Verse

"Moshe came and told the people everything *ADONAI* had said, including all the rulings. The people answered with one voice: "We will obey every word *ADONAI* has spoken.'"

Exodus 18:20 CJB

Did You Know?

Hur, who is spoken of with Moshe, was Miryam's (Miriam) son.

Mishpatim   Exodus 21:1-24:18 Activity Sheet

Rumors

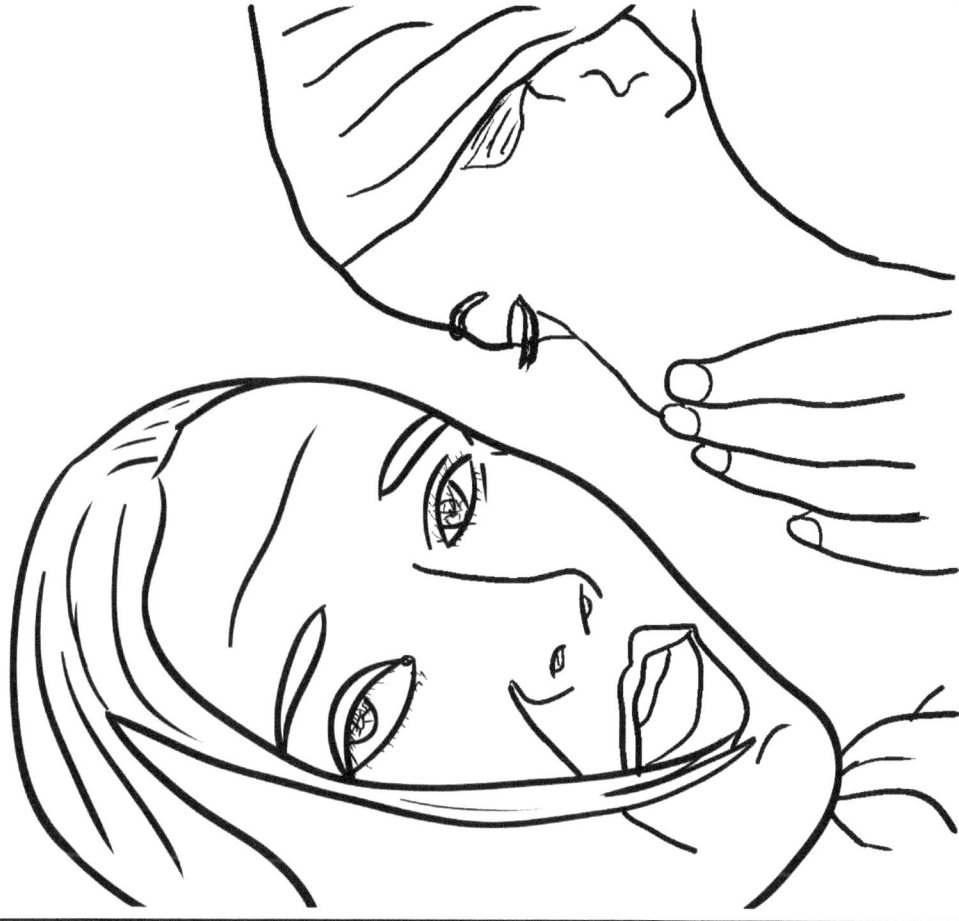

"You are not to repeat false rumors; do not join hands with the wicked by offering perjured testimony." Exodus 23:1 CJB

ADONAI Justice System

ADONAI is fair and just. Match these actions with their consequences. For help read Exodus 21:26,33,37(22:1)* , 22:4(5)

Blinding a servant

Leaving a well open, and an animal falling in

Steeling a sheep

Letting an animal eat another's field

Pay 4 times as much as the worth

Pay from your own produce

Set them free

Pay replacement money

* the verses in brackets are the same verses in other translations.

Yirmeyahu
(Jeremiah) 34:8-22, 33:25-26

Haftara 18 (Prophets)

Memory Verse

"At the end of seven years every one of you is to set free his brother Hebrew who has been sold to you and has served you six years. You are to let him go free from you..."
Jeremiah 34:14 CJB

Did You Know?

There are more people in slavery today than ever before.

Promise

Jeremiah 33:26

"...For I will cause their captives to come back, and I will show them compassion."

STORY SUMMARY

A Broken Covenant: ADONAI, through Yirmeyahu, tells of the consequences that will follow for those who broke the covenant they had recently made to set their fellow Hebrew slaves free. Many who made the covenant let their slaves free, but then changed their mind and forced them to come back. The last passage reminds us that although there were consequences for this, forgiveness and restoration would follow.

WORD FOCUS

Chophshi: 'Free'. Which means to be released from something that had once held you. To be free from sin means sin no longer is in control of you.

MAIN MESSAGE

Slavery has never been ADONAI's plan, but was permitted for a time of seven years. It is dangerous to have such power and control over another person. The full picture of being in bondage and being freed is one that ADONAI wants us to understand. We are in bondage to sin, but there is freedom in Him.

FREEDOM   JUSTICE   COMPASSION

Yirmeyahu 34:8-22 Activity Sheet

Freedom

Set these out of place letters free. Write the freed letters in the spaces below to reveal the command ADONAI gave Isra'el in Jeremiah 34:8 CJB.

Tshis woerd ctame tot Yirmeyahuh

freom ADONAIH afeter kbing

Tzidkiyahur haed mawde sa clovenant

witha vall tehe peosple fin

Yerushalayimr toe emancipatee the!m.

— — — — — — — — — — — — —

— — — — — — — — — — — — —

Slaves

"Everyone who had a male or female slave who was Hebrew was to let him go free; none was to keep as his slave a fellow Jew." Jeremiah 34:9 CJB

Hebrews   B'rit Hadashah 18
13:1-24   (Newer Testament)

STORY SUMMARY

Commands to love: Believers are encouraged to love each other, honour ADONAI and marriage partners, be careful what is believed, remember Yeshua's sacrifice and promise, respect leaders and keep praying.

WORD FOCUS

Shema: 'Hear'. This means to listen. It is also connected to 'obey'. It is an action word that involves thoughtful consideration, not mindlessly following something.

MEMORY VERSE

"Remember your leaders, those who spoke G-d's message to you. Reflect on the results of their way of life, and imitate their trust". Hebrews 13:7

MAIN MESSAGE

Our Parasha listed fifty-three rulings ADONAI wanted us to keep that are still relevant. Hebrews lists more ways to live that will bring life. All of these rulings focus on how we will love each other and ADONAI. Hebrews confirms we should respect our leaders and those in authority. Manners is good in every situation.

PROMISE

"But don't forget to be friendly to outsiders; for in so doing, some people, without knowing it, have entertained angels." Hebrews 13:1-24 CJB

DID YOU KNOW?

Many believe that Shaul (Paul) wrote Hebrews, but nobody is completely sure.

Hebrews 13:1-24 Activity Sheet

Rules of Life

We all need rules of some kind in life. Sometimes these rules are different in different places. What rules do you have in your family? Do you have different or extra rules in another place such as school?

School/other place Rules

Home Rules

Money

$ $ $ $

My Want list

"Keep your lives free from the love of money; and be satisfied with what you have; for G-d himself has said, 'I will never fail you or abandon you.'"

Hebrews 13:5 CJB

Parasha 19

Memory Verse

"Tell the people of Isra'el to take up a collection for me— accept a contribution from anyone who whole-heartedly wants to give."

Exodus 25:2 CJB

Did You Know?

The tent of the Tabernacle had four layers.

1. Fine Linen
2. Goat's Hair
3. Red ram's skin
4. Marine animal skin (or something similar that has been hard to define)

תרומה Terumah (contribution) Exodus 25:1-27:19

STORY SUMMARY

ADONAI gives Moshe(Moses) instructions on how to build the Tabernacle:

ADONAI asks the people to donate the things needed to build a tabernacle. This tabernacle would be the home of the commandments He was about to send, and ADONAI Himself would dwell there among them. He wanted them to give from a grateful heart. ADONAI then gives very detailed directions on how each item is to be made.

WORD FOCUS

Mishkan (Tabernacle): This place was to be ADONAI's holy dwelling. What is holiness? Kadosh (holy) means separate, out of the ordinary, different – even unique.

MAIN MESSAGE

It was not for Himself that ADONAI wanted a tabernacle. It was for us, so we could have a closer experience with Him and no longer be lost or slaves. He wanted to bless us and make us holy, set apart for Him. Today through the Ruach HaKodesh (Holy Spirit) His tabernacle is within us. He does not force us to worship Him but He invites us be part of His divine blessing. When we accept ADONAI and follow His ways we are to be different from the world. Not the same. This is sometimes hard when our human nature tells us we don't want to be different.

LOVE of ADONAI	FREE WILL	PURE HEART	SET APART

Promise

Exodus 25:9 CJB

"They are to make me a sanctuary, so that I may live among them."

Terumah Exodus 25:1-27:19 Activity Sheet

Menorah

These cups must also have buds and petals. Put a bud under each pair of branches that goes out from the lampstand....:Then make seven small oil lamps and put them on the menorah. They will give light to the area in front of the menorah. The wick trimmers and trays must be made of pure gold.

Exodus 25:31-38

CJB

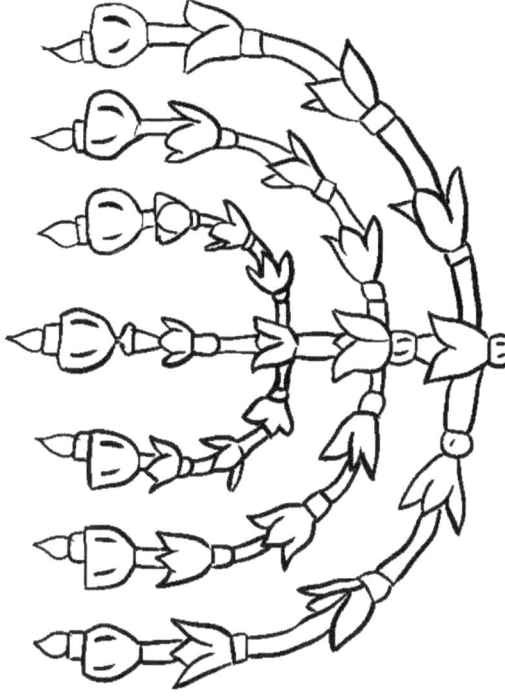

Hammer pure gold to make a menorah. It's base, stand , flower like cups, buds and petals must be all joined together in one piece. The menorah must have three branches on one side and three branches on the other. Each branch must have three cups shaped like almond flowers on it. Each cup must have a bud and a petal. And there must be four more cups made like almond flowers on the lampstand itself.

Mishkan

Cut out (or draw a line from) the items and stick them in their right place in the sanctuary. See how many you can get right.

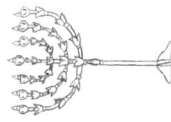

Ark of the Covenant

Altar of incense

Menorah   Table of showbread

Bronze Altar

Bronze Basin

M'lakim Alef

(1 Kings 5:26-6:13)

Haftara 19 (Prophets)

Memory Verse

"ADONAI gave Shlomo wisdom as He had promised him and there was peace between Hiram and Shlomo."

(1 Kings 5:26) CJB

Did You Know?

The cost to build the Temple in today's money is about 3-6 billion dollars!

Promise

1 Kings 6:12-13 CJB

"Concerning this house: if you will live according to my regulations, follow my rulings and observe all my mitzvot (commands) and live by them, then I will establish with you my promise that I made to David your father— I will live in it among the people of Isra'el, and I will not abandon my people Isra'el."

STORY SUMMARY

Shlomo (Solomon) Builds a Temple for ADONAI: Now that the people are in their own land they can build a temple that does not get moved around. King Shlomo was a very wise king. He put aside his differences and enlisted the help of Hiram. Then, he organised the workforce and got to work on building a temple made from stone.

WORD FOCUS

Mitzvot: 'The commands of ADONAI'. It is also used to describe an act of kindness.

Bet HaMikdash: is the name for Shlomo's Temple. A 'bet' is a house. 'Mikdash' comes from kadosh, meaning holy. In the Tanach, it is referred to as the 'House' in which ADONAI especially dwells, the place where ADONAI and the Jewish people met in holiness.

MAIN MESSAGE

Again here, just as in the building of the tabernacle, ADONAI is only interested in people serving Him wholeheartedly and being obedient to Him. It didn't matter how much money was spent on making it or how beautiful it was, if the people didn't truly want the relationship with ADONAI, He would not protect it from enemies. Today it is the same. ADONAI will live in you if you truly want Him.

OBEY   SERVE   LOVE

M'lakim Alef (1 Kings 5:26-6:13) Activity Sheet

Temple

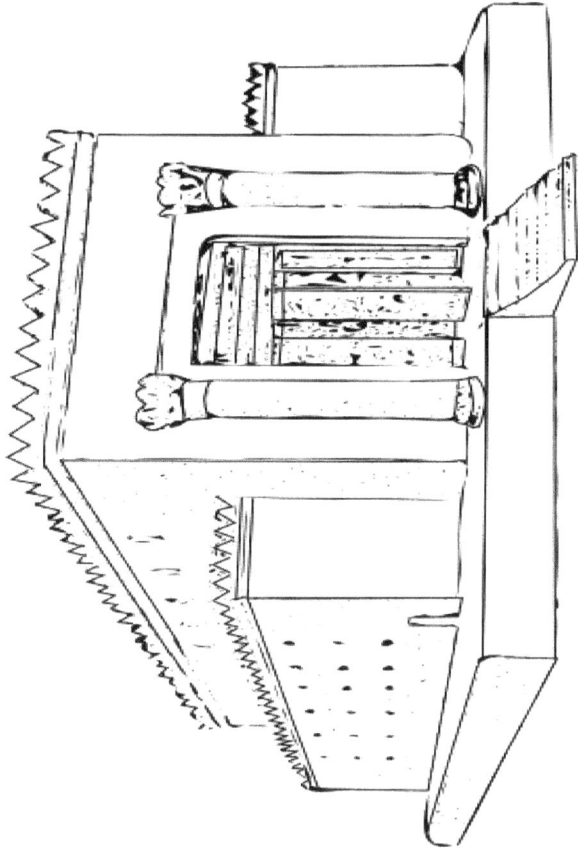

"Then he (David) called his son Solomon and instructed him to build a temple for ADONAI of Isra'el".

1 Chronicles 22:6 NLT

Building the walls

Unscramble the memory verse on the wall stones in the correct order. One word is done for you.

had was between gave promised and Shlomo and ADONAI Wisdom 1 Kings 5:26 Hiram there he Shlomo him as peace.

between

Hebrews   B'rit Hadashah 19

8:1-6; 9:22-24;10:1 (Newer Testament)

STORY SUMMARY

Our High Priest: The Tabernacle was a replica of the Sanctuary in Heaven where Yeshua is the high priest (cohen-gadol). Making things clean and pure came through blood. A priest had to offer a gift and a sacrifice. Yeshua did this once and for all when He died and offered His own blood.

WORD FOCUS

HaG'dulah: This word describes ADONAI as "the Greatness and the Majesty". It does not say He is great but is THE GREATNESS. There is no words to describe how truly great He is. All other things that are called great can't compare.

MEMORY VERSE

"For the Messiah has entered the Holiest place which is not man made... but into Heaven itself in order to appear now on our behalf in the very presence of ADONAI".

Hebrews 9:24 CJB

MAIN MESSAGE

Because of what Yeshua did we no longer need to sacrifice animals for sin. His blood has the power to cleanse us and make us pure. His temple is now in us and He is our high priest, our gateway to ADONAI. Through His righteousness we are made righteous. If we stay faithful to Him, He will stay faithful to us and keep His promise to be together forever.

PROMISE

"And this is the promise that He has promised us, even eternal life." 1 John 2:25 CJB

DID YOU KNOW?

In 70 CE, the Second Temple was destroyed and there has not been a another one since.

Our High Priest Activity Sheet

Writing in Hebrew

In Hebrew, words are read the opposite way to English. For example if you were to write the word 'cheese' it would be written starting from the right 'eseehc'.

The word for High Priest is Cohen-gadol

גדול כהן

Now you try to write it.

Alef (silent)	Bet (B/V)	Gimel (G)	Dalet (D)	He (H)	Vav (V)
Zayin (Z)	Chet (Ch)	Tet (T)	Yud (Y)	Kaf (K/Kh)	Khaf (Kh)
Lamed (L)	Mem (M)	Mem (M)	Nun (N)	Nun (N)	Samech (S)
Ayin (silent)	Peh (P/F)	Feh (F)	Tsadeh (Ts)	Tsadeh (Ts)	Qof (Q)
Resh (R)	Shin (Sh/S)	Tav (T)			

Yeshua our High Priest

"Therefore since we have a great high priest who has passed through to the highest heaven, Yeshua, the son of ADONAI, let us hold firm to what we know is true." Hebrews 4:14 (CJB)

Parasha 20

פרשת תצוה

Tetzaveh (You are to order) Exodus 27:20-30:10

Memory Verse

"You are to order the people of Isra'el to bring you pure oil of pounded olives for the light, and keep a lamp burning continually."

Exodus 25:2 CJB

Keep your light burning continually by staying in touch with ADONAI through prayer, bible study and the power of the Ruach.

Promise

Exodus 29:43 CJB

"There I will meet with the people of Isra'el and the place will be consecrated by my glory."

Did You Know?

Colours have meaning in the Bible. For example, purple symbolises royalty.

1 Peter 2:9 tells of a 'Royal Priesthood.'

STORY SUMMARY

ADONAI Appoints the Priesthood: ADONAI chooses Aaron and his sons to serve as priests.

What to Wear: ADONAI gives instructions on what clothes the priests are to wear; what they are to look like and the colour they will be.

How to Begin: ADONAI tells how to bless and cleanse the priests for the job they will do.

Altar of Incense: ADONAI gives instructions on how to build the altar of incense. He also tells how and when it is to be used.

WORD FOCUS

Lehorot and **Lehavdil:** The key verbs of priesthood, meaning to instruct and distinguish. To distinguish is to set apart. ADONAI is using the system of the priesthood to set His people apart and make them pure.

MAIN MESSAGE

ADONAI wanted to communicate with His people. This was not possible without a mediator. (someone to speak or act on behalf of) This priesthood was set up to be the mediator between ADONAI and His people. Everything ADONAI set up had a reason. As we study these reasons we can know more of Him and His plan to save us.

DESIRE of ADONAI   KNOWLEDGE of His plan   CONFIDENCE in His plan

Colour this High Priest's garments according to ADONAI's instructions.
Either colour it according to the letter shown or the instruction given.

Gold Bands

Black Onyx Stones on each shoulder set in Gold.

Colour this tunic in various patterns with gold, blue, purple and scarlet and white (to represent linen)

This is an alternating pattern of pomegranates and bells. So one red then one gold and repeat until the end

Make the outside gold

B/G	Y	R
W	B	LGr
P	RB	O
Br	Bl	Pi

COLOUR KEY

B = Blue

Bl = Black

Br = Brown

B/G = Blue Green

G = Gold

LGr = Light Green

O = Orange

P = Purple

Pi = Pink

R = Red

RB = Rainbow

W = White

Y = Yellow

Yechezkel

(Ezekiel) 43:10-27

Haftara 20 (Prophets)

Promise

Ezekiel 43:7 CJB

"…This is the place for my throne, the place for the soles of my feet, where I will live among the people of Isra'el forever!"

Memory Verse

"…describe this house to the house of Isra'el so that they will be ashamed of their crimes…"

Ezekiel 43:10 CJB

Did You Know?

One of the famous Jewish principles of Chazal says:

Whoever believes in the advent of Messiah will be saved.

STORY SUMMARY

Ezekiel's a Vision of the Future Temple: Ezekiel is shown the details of the future temple. ADONAI shows him so that the people will be ashamed and come back to ADONAI. If His people come back to Him, ADONAI promises they will have a part in this new temple where He will dwell with them forever. He wanted them to know exactly what it would look like.

WORD FOCUS

Yechezkel: 'ADONAI Strengthens'. This fits the message of hope to Isra'el Ezekiel was given. Even though Isra'el was in exile for their sins, ADONAI had not forgotten them. If they said they were sorry and changed their ways, ADONAI would accept them and they would again see His glory.

MAIN MESSAGE

ADONAI provided hope and strength at a time when the people were down. They were not sure if He would accept them again since they sinned and were sent out of their land. Sometimes, when we do things wrong, we too wonder if ADONAI or others will still love us or forgive us. We often feel relief to know we are still loved and forgiven and are part of His future plan. ADONAI wanted the people of Isra'el to feel this way too when they heard the message to be encouraged and faithful.

REPENT   RETURN   FORIVENESS   STRENGTH   HOPE

Yechezkel 43:10-27 Activity Sheet

Ezekiel's Vision

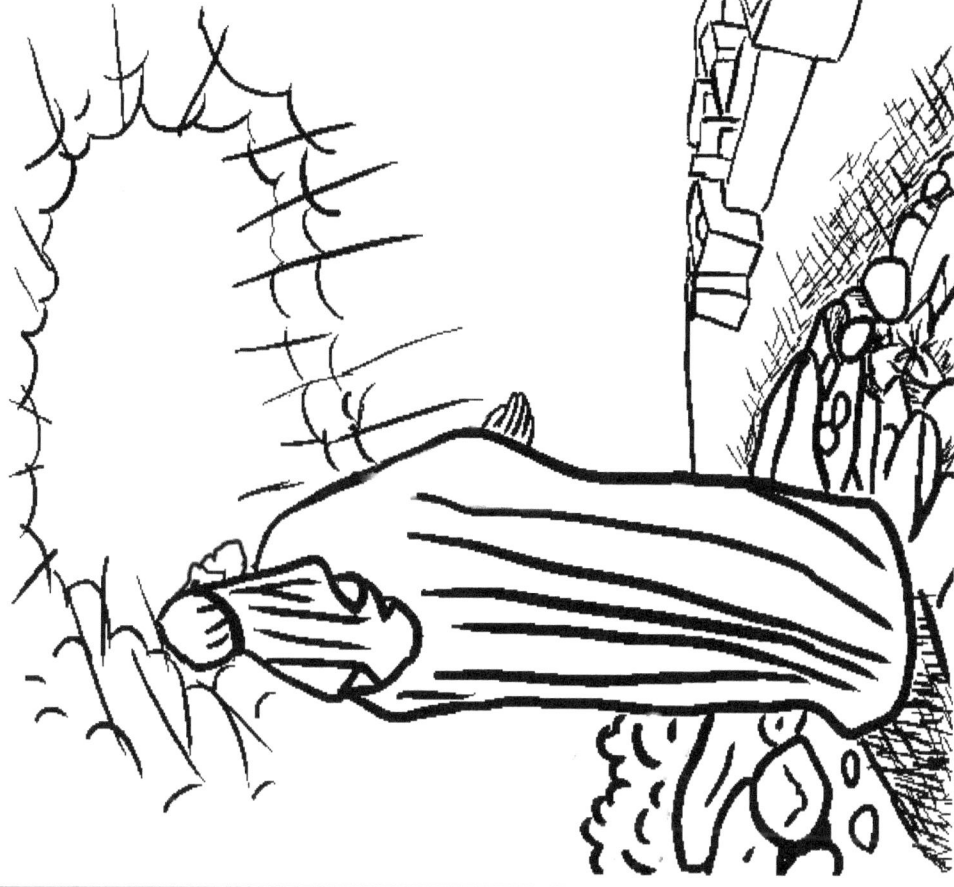

In vision, G-d bought me into the land of Isra'el and put me down on a very high mountain..." Ezekiel 40:2 CJB

Following Instructions

ADONAI instructed Ezekiel how to draw the Temple. Do you think you can follow instructions to draw something in the box below?

1. In the top of the square, in the middle draw a big triangle. Make it come about half way down the box.

2. Under the triangle, draw a slightly smaller square to the bottom of the box.

3. In the middle of the square at the bottom draw a tall rectangle, with a small circle in the middle to the left.

4. Draw two small squares above the rectangle, one near the right edge and one near the left edge. What have you drawn?

John 1:1-5, 8:12 B'rit Hadashah 20

Isaiah 11:1-3 (Newer Testament)

STORY SUMMARY

Yeshua is the light of the world: In John, Yeshua says He is the light of the world. He is the word of ADONAI. Isaiah predicted His coming and said "the spirit of the LORD shall rest upon him."

WORD FOCUS

Shemen: 'Oil'. Oil was used every day as fuel for indoor lights. There was no electricity. When oil was in great supply, people were happy and things were good. Oil was used to anoint specific people for their tasks. The sick were also anointed.

Masah: 'To apply oil'. The title, Mashiach (Messiah) 'The Anointed One' comes from this word.

MEMORY VERSE

"In the beginning was the word, and the word was with G-d, and the word was G-d. He was in the beginning with G-d."

John 1:1-2

MAIN MESSAGE

Exodus 27:20 is about the oil and keeping the menorah burning. The menorah's seven lamps filled with holy oil represent the Mashiach 'anointed one' filled with the seven gifts of the Ruach Hashem (Holy Spirit). The six branches of the menorah come in pairs and represent pairs of gifts. These are: Wisdom and Understanding, Counsel and Might, Knowledge and Fear of ADONAI. The Ruach Hashem is in the centre of the six branches. Yeshua is the Mashiach, the one represented by this menorah, and also the mediator.

PROMISE

"Again Yeshua spoke to them, saying, 'I am the light of the world. Whoever follows me will not walk in darkness, but will have the light of life.'" John 8:12

DID YOU KNOW?

An oil lamp such as used in bible times lasted all night. Olive oil only burns on the wick. If it spills or falls over it will go out. The oil itself will not burn, so it is one of the safest ways to have fire. ADONAI knew what He was doing when He said to use it.

John 1:1-5, 8:12 Activity Sheet

Light the Way

Light up the path for the lost sheep to find her way home. Follow the lighter letters to find the hidden message. Write it in the spaces below.

W	A	R	S	F	G		Y
U		E	Q	Z	P	E	T
J	I		O		D		H
B			K	L	X	C	V
N	S		K	T	I	B	W
M		R	M	P	O	C	A	H
Q	O		R	X	Y	Z	U
	G	H	V	W	T	R	E	F

_ _ _ _ _ _ _ _ _ _ _ _ _

Yeshua, Light of the World

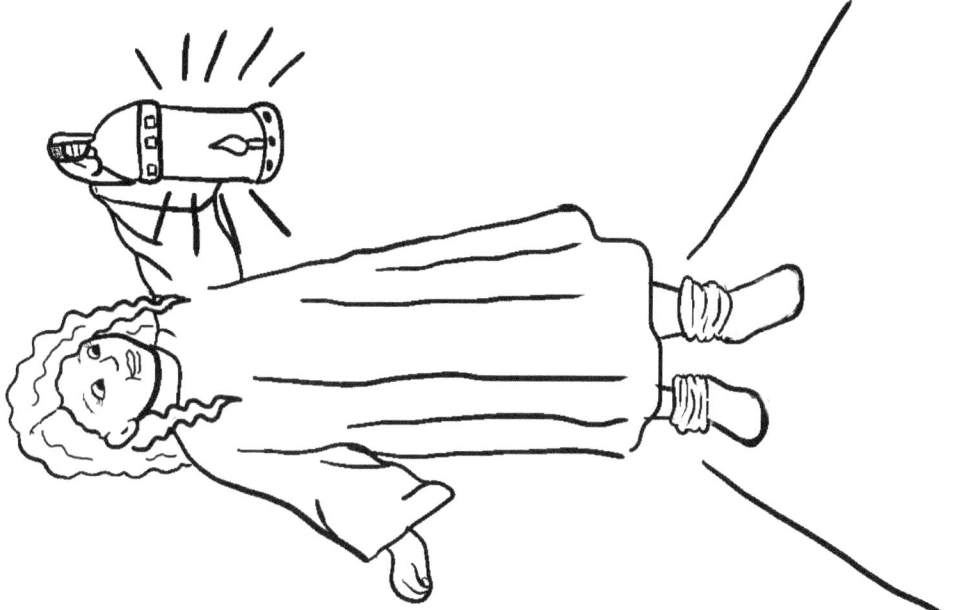

"Your word is a lamp to my feet and a light to my path."
Psalms 119:105 ESV

Parasha 21

פרשת כי תשא Ki Tisa (When you take) Exodus 30:11-34:35

Memory Verse

"...I have endowed all the craftsmen with the wisdom to make everything I have ordered you."

Exodus 31:6 CJB

If ADONAI has asked you to do something, you can trust that He will give you the ability to do it. He gives creative gifts to be used to glorify His name.

STORY SUMMARY

ADONAI further Instructs Moshe(Moses): ADONAI instructs Moshe to take a census. After this he is instructed to have a wash basin, some holy oil and some holy incense made.

Moshe Receives the Covenant: ADONAI reminds Isra'el to keep Shabbat. This is the sign of the covenant He is making with them. Then ADONAI calls Moshe up the mountain to receive the covenant. When he takes a long time to come back, the people make a golden calf to worship. Moshe drops and brakes the covenant when he sees the people worshiping the calf. ADONAI is not happy with the people but Moshe begs for mercy and ADONAI spares many lives. Moshe pitches a tent outside the camp. Here he speaks to ADONAI through a pillar cloud while in the tent. Because Moshe broke the stones he needs to go back up the mountain for another set. ADONAI tells Moshe His name but does not show His face. Moshe comes down glowing, with the stone tablets.

WORD FOCUS

Kavod: Glory. This is a military word for heavy and slender armour, meaning power and might. When Moshe asked ADONAI to show His glory, he was asking Him to show His power and might.

MAIN MESSAGE

ADONAI made every effort to have a relationship with His people. By 'changing His mind', ADONAI showed that He was all about relationship. He was, and still is, willing to forgive us so we can have a relationship with Him and be called His covenant people. ADONAI always makes a way for us.

OBEDIANCE   FAITHFULNESS   RELATIONSHIP

Promise

Exodus 31:13 CJB

"...You are to observe my shabbats, for this is a sign between me and and you through all your generations; so that you will know that I am ADONAI, who set you apart for me."

Did You Know?

Money was taken for the census so the people could be counted. Each coin represented one person.

Ki Tisa Exodus 30:11-34:35 Activity Sheet

"When Moshe came down from Mount Sinai with the two tablets of the testimony in his hand, he did not realise that the skin on his face was sending out rays of light as a result of talking with ADONAI." Exodus 34:29 CJB

Attributes of ADONAI Word Search

Find the attributes of ADONAI as He told to Moshe in Exodus 34:6-7.

```
C M Z Q X Z C S Y M Y L L P L
A O L O O X U L A V O N U A O
O T M B R O S U E V T X F R N
W I Q P I N T N I A X H I D G
N Z J C A H L N T Z N B C O S
N O A X O S G " M G W S R N U
T R Y R K O S M F N N W E S F
G Q I G N I V I G R O F M S F
D T W T R K F H O P E G U J E
Y T R U T H F U L N B W B G R
S E I V B E N A O X A C O F I
L D N I K U V W E Z M T N P N
K Q O P R R I Z W P G A E H G
T P Y Z O B H X E C P X O C P
N K X G E P Y N T Z W Y E Z G
```

Compassionate

Powerful

Authority

Merciful

Gracious

Longsuffering

Loving

Kind

Truthful

Forgiving

Cleanses

Pardons

M'lakim Alef

(1 Kings) 18:1-39

Haftara 21 (Prophets)

Memory Verse

"Eliyahu took twelve stones in keeping with the number of tribes of the sons of Yakov (Jacob), to whom the word of ADONAI had come, saying, 'your name is to be Isra'el.'"

1 Kings 18:31 CJB

Did You Know?

Eliyahu did not die, but was taken up by ADONAI.

STORY SUMMARY

Eliyahu (Elijah) Shows Himself to King Achav: Eliyahu has been hiding because the king blamed him for the famine, but ADONAI tells Elijah to show himself to the king.

Elijah challenges the gods of Baal: Eliyahu tells the priests of Baal to build an altar with a sacrifice to Baal, and Eliyahu builds an altar with a sacrifice to ADONAI. Eliyahu challenges the priests of Baal to call on their gods. The one who answered would be the true G-d. The gods of Baal didn't answer, but ADONAI rained fire down and destroyed the whole Altar.

WORD FOCUS

Yisroel (Isra'el): 'The straight of G-d.' 'Yasher' means straight and 'El' means G-d. Ya'akov's name was changed from 'on the heal of' to this after he overcame. This shows an important relationship between ADONAI and His people for all time that cannot be separated.

MAIN MESSAGE

This sacrifice that was made outside the Temple showed that ADONAI was G-d, not only in Jerusalem but everywhere. It also showed that He wanted a relationship with Isra'el outside of the Temple too. Even though they had turned against Him, He still came looking for them. ADONAI wanted them to be sorry and come back. He wants that relationship with you, too.

FAITHFULNESS of ADONAI   RELATIONSHIP   POWER   FORGIVENESS

Promise

1 Kings 18:1 CJB

"Go, present yourself to Achav, and I will send rain down on the land."

M'lakim Alef 1 Kings 18:1-39 Activity Sheet

Fire from Heaven

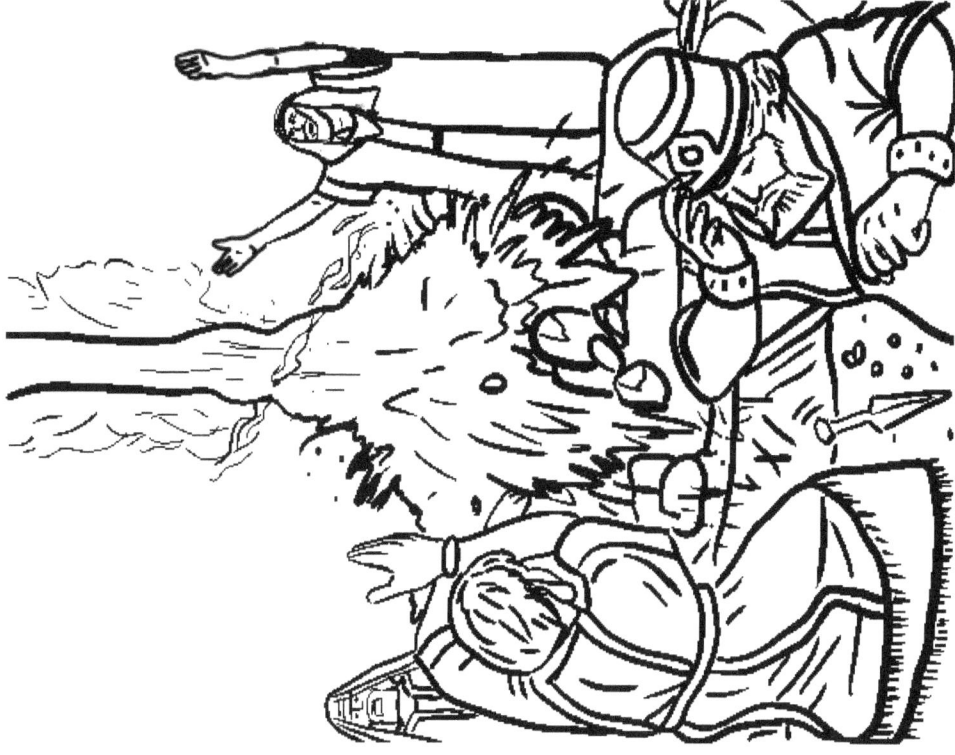

"Then the fire of ADONAI fell, it consumed the burnt offering, the wood, the stones and the dust; and it licked up the water in the trench." 1 Kings 18:38 CJB

The Twelve Tribes Of Isra'el

Unscramble the English names of the tribes written in the altar stones.
For help see Genesis 46:8-26.

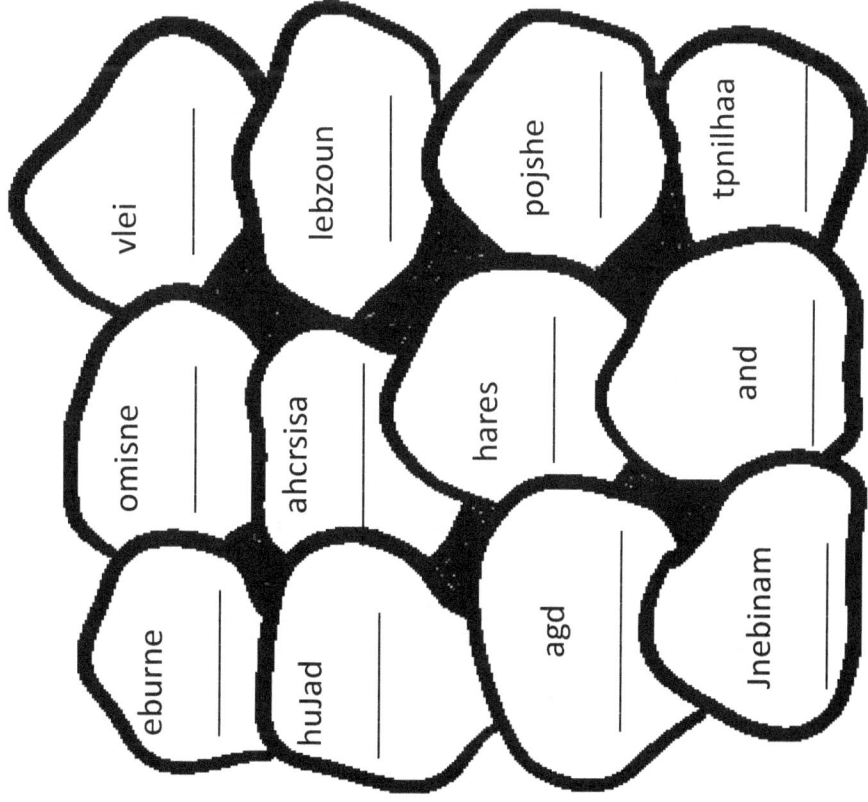

vlei _____

lebzoun _____

pojshe _____

tpnilhaa _____

omisne _____

ahcrsisa _____

hares _____

and _____

eburne _____

huJad _____

agd _____

Jnebinam _____

Luke
B'rit Hadashah 21
21:1 - 4 (Newer Testament)

STORY SUMMARY

The Rich and the Poor Givers: Yeshua is teaching at the Temple. He sees the rich bring offerings and a poor woman bring an offering. Although the rich give more, Yeshua sees the hearts of all givers and praises the offering of the poor woman higher than all the offerings of the rich.

WORD FOCUS

Tikkun Olam: Repairing the World. This speaks of social responsibility. In Luke 20:46 Yeshua speaks of teachers who want to be great but cause hard times on the poor. The widow in our story should have been looked after by her community. How can you help look after your community?

MEMORY VERSE

"For they, out of their wealth have contributed money they could easily spare; but she, out of her poverty, has given all she had to live on." Luke 21:4

MAIN MESSAGE

Although she offered her last coin, the widow gave with faith, trust and a willing heart. The rich gave more but it was not out of a grateful heart. There was no personal sacrifice. Maybe they did it to be seen by others or maybe gave only because it was a rule. Our promise and Matthew 19:23-24 tell us that wealth does not make you great in the Kingdom. Serving ADONAI with a willing heart makes you great. This is especially true if you are willing to give up something to serve Him. This might be: time, possessions, pocket money or even being popular with friends.

PROMISE

"But whoever would be great among you must be your servant." Matthew 20:26

DID YOU KNOW?

The copper coins the widow gave would probably have been the same as two one dollar coins today.

Luke 21:1-4 Activity Sheet

The Poor Widow

"Yeshua looked up, and He watched the rich placing their gifts into the Temple offering–box, He also saw a poor widow put in two coins." Luke 21:1-2 CJB

Make Me a Servant

Draw a picture of you doing something nice for someone.

שמות ויקהל # Uayakhel (He assembled) Exodus 35:1-38:20

Promise

Exodus 35:30-31 CJB

"See ADONAI has singled out Betzalel ... He has filled him with the spirit of ADONAI— with wisdom, understanding and knowledge concerning every kind of artistry."

Parasha 22

Memory Verse

"And they came, everyone whose heart stirred him and everyone whose spirit made him willing and brought ADONAI's offering..."

Exodus 35:21 CJB

Did you Know?

Betzalel's grandfather, Chur, was killed trying to stop the building of the golden calf. ADONAI honoured his faithfulness.

(Rabbi Avi Geller)

STORY SUMMARY

Isra'el's Obligation: Moshe (Moses) assembles the people together to tell them again what ADONAI wants them to do as His covenant people. He starts with the Shabbat, the sign of the covenant, and reminds them to keep it. Moshe then reminds them of what ADONAI wants the Tabernacle and it's furnishings to be built with and who will make them. Several times it is repeated that ADONAI wants them to give from a willing heart.

WORD FOCUS

Shabbat: 'Ceasing' or 'stopping.' ADONAI reminded the people about the Shabbat, first because He wanted them to know that even though He had a special work for them to do in building the Tabernacle, they were still to stop and rest on the Shabbat, as He stopped and rested from the things He had made.

MAIN MESSAGE

The Shabbat was at the centre of Isra'el's life and worship. Ahad HaAm commented, "More than the Jews have kept the Shabbat, Shabbat has kept the Jews." ADONAI wants to bless us and make it possible for us to carry out His work. Just like Betzalel and the people who gave up their things for the Tabernacle, He will send us His spirit so we can do the things He has asked us to do. What special gift or talent can you serve ADONAI with?

ETERNAL COVENANT   WILLING HEART   SERVE   BE SPIRIT LED

56

This picture shows what the Mishkan (Tabernacle) may have looked like if you could see through walls. It is not broken but drawn so you can see what is inside. The lines you see on the tent cover represent the four layers, and the area dividers are curtains

Fill in the missing words of the 4th commandment. If you need help you can find it in Exodus 20: 8-11 CJB

"_____ the day _____, to set it apart for _____. You have _____ days to _____ and do all your _____, but the _____ day is a _____ for _____ your _____. On it you shall _____ do any kind of _____ — not you, your _____, or daughter, not your _____ or female _____, not your livestock, and not the _____ staying with you who is inside the _____ to your property. For in six days _____ made _____ and earth, the sea, and _____ in them; but on the seventh _____ He rested. This is why ADONAI _____ the day, Shabbat, and _____ it for Himself."

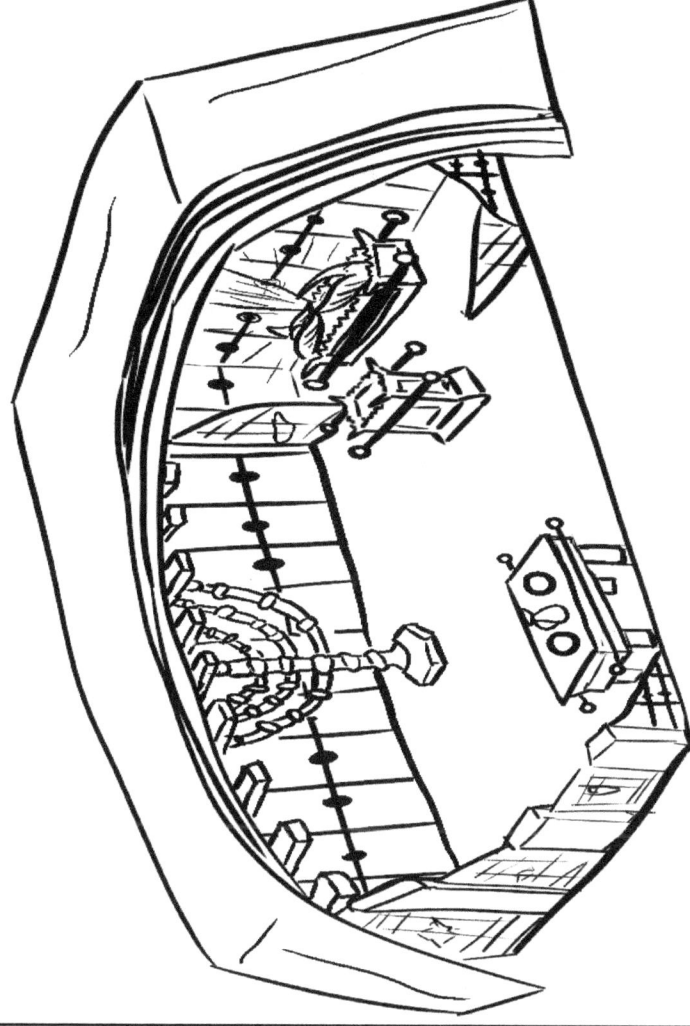

M'lakim Alef

1 Kings 7:13-26

STORY SUMMARY

The Bronze Items for the Temple: Shlomo (Solomon) sends for Hiram the bronze-worker, to help make the Temple. Hiram is recognised to have wisdom, understanding and skill.

WORD FOCUS

Yakhin: Yah Establishes. **Boaz:** Strength.

These were the names given to the pillars of the Temple. They are said to have represented King Shlomo (Yakin) and King David (Boaz), who also represent the Messiah.

MAIN MESSAGE

It was important to get the right person for the job. Shlomo knew Hiram was good at what he did. He only wanted the best for ADONAI's house. Like Betzalel, Hiram was blessed by ADONAI with creative talent and wisdom to use the talent well. When we do things, we should do our best work and take pride in it. We should also look for ways to serve ADONAI. This will be an example to others of our character.

BE A BLESSING   **SERVE**   **DILIGENCE**

Haftara 22 (Prophets)

Memory Verse

"Whatever task comes your way, do it with all your strength..."

Ecclesiastes 9:10 CJB

Did You Know?

The pillars Hiram crafted for the Temple were just under three stories high.

Promise

Proverbs 22:1 ESV

"A good name is to be chosen rather than great riches, and favour is better than silver or gold."

M'lakim Alef (1 Kings) 7:13-26 Activity Sheet

"He made two bronze columns, each one thirty-one and a half feet high and twenty-one feet in circumference." 1 Kings 7:15

ADONAI's House

2 Chronicles 2:6 says that ADONAI cannot be contained in a house. Draw a picture, or pictures, of the place, or places, you feel most close to ADONAI.

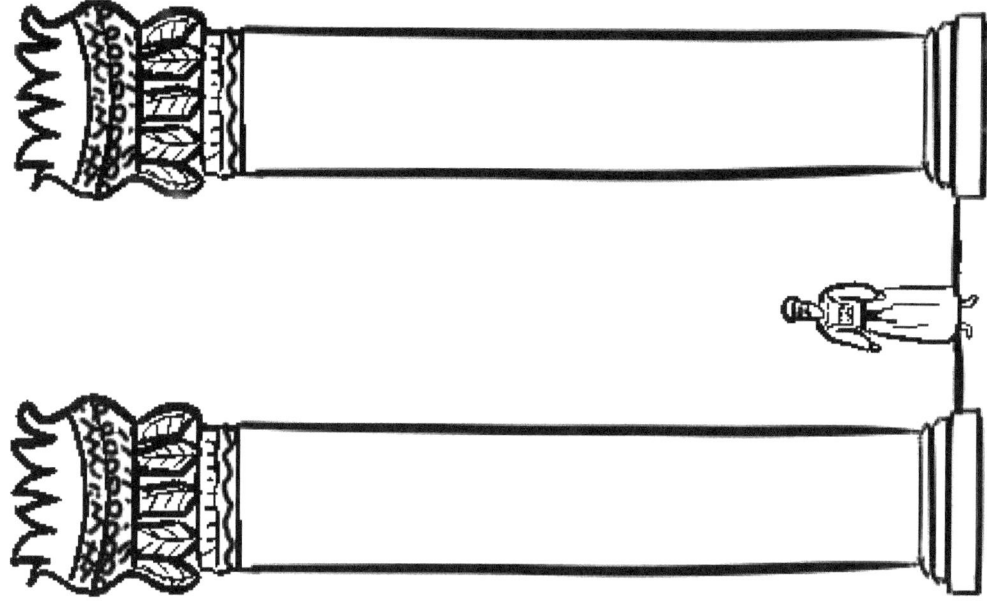

Matthew 24:1-20

B'rit Hadashah 22
(Newer Testament)

STORY SUMMARY

Times to Come: Yeshua warns His disciples that times will be hard before He comes back. He also tells them that many people will be tricked into following false beliefs by false leaders, either pretending to be the Messiah, or on the Messiah's side. He describes the conditions just before the end and mentions the Shabbat.

WORD FOCUS

Olam Ha ba: The world to come.

Olam Hazeh: The life we live now and the world we know. Yeshua was talking to His disciples about the end of the Olam Hazeh.

MEMORY VERSE

"Pray that you will not have to escape in the winter or on Shabbat." Matthew 24:20 CJB

MAIN MESSAGE

The law of ADONAI doesn't change. The Shabbat will be as important to Him at the end of time as it was at the start of time. Yeshua's warning is for us today. There are some who teach that the Law of ADONAI is no longer important to Him. When times get hard He promises, if we stay faithful, He will be with us.

PROMISE

"But whoever holds out to the end will be delivered."
Matthew 24: 13 CJB

DID YOU KNOW?

Matthew used the Tanakh, to show that Yeshua fulfilled the criteria for the Messiah more than 130 times.

Matthew 24:1-20 Activity Sheet

The Sign

What is the sign? Fill in the missing letters then unscramble the word they make to find the sign.

" T_is is is to _e a sign _etween me _nd you for _ll your genera_ion_. "

The Sign: _ _ _

Yeshua on the Mount of Olives

"When He was sitting on the Mount of Olives, His talmidim came to Him privately. "Tell us," they said, "when will all these things happen? And what will be the sign that You are coming, and that the olam hazeh is ending?" Matthew 24: 3 CJB

Parasha 23
פקודי Pekudei

(Accounts) Exodus 38:21-40:38

Promise

Deut 28:3 CJB

"All the following blessings will be yours in abundance if you will do what ADONAI your G-d says."

STORY SUMMARY

Isra'el follows ADONAI's Instructions: The Tabernacle and all the things in it are made just as ADONAI has instructed. Betzalel and Oholiav are blessed with the skills and knowledge needed for the task. The people work together and bring the materials. Soon everything is complete. The Tabernacle and the priests are purified, and the presence of ADONAI comes down as a cloud and leads them.

WORD FOCUS

Avodah: 'Service to ADONAI!' This word is used instead of the usual word for 'work' when referring to the building of the Tabernacle. This is because it was a direct instruction from ADONAI in service to Him. Through this, the people learnt that ADONAI also wanted them as servants, not just Moshe (Moses). ADONAI wanted the people to make a house for Him together.

MAIN MESSAGE

ADONAI does not work only through one person. He works through a community of believers. When you are obedient and faithful to Him, He can use you. Just as when the Isra'elites were faithful, ADONAI was able to inspire them directly and show them His favour. Each person has their part to play in the community and every role is important.

OBEY   SERVE   BLESSINGS

Memory Verse

"The people of Isra'el did all the work just as ADONAI had ordered Moshe... And Moshe blessed them."

Exodus 39: 42-43 CJB

Did You Know?

Betzalel's name meant 'in the shadow of ADONAI' and 'When ADONAI spoke to me.'

Every one of us can be used like Betzalel if we are willing and faithful.

62

40:38 Activity Sheet

"Then the cloud covered the tent of meeting, and the glory of ADONAI filled the Tabernacle." Exodus 40:34 CJB

Help this community work together to discover ADONAI's promise to the people if they were faithful to Him. Put the message in the right order by rewriting the words on their same shape below.

M'lakhim Alef

(1 Kings) 7:51-8:21

STORY SUMMARY

The Temple is Finished and Blessed: Hiram had finished the bronze work and Shlomo (Solomon) had finished the gold work. Shlomo calls all the leaders together and brings the Ark of the Covenant in to the Temple.

The Glory of ADONAI Fills the Temple: After the priests leave the Holy Place, the presence of ADONAI filled the Temple as a thick cloud. It is so thick the priests can not stand.

WORD FOCUS

Aron Habrit: 'Ark of the Covenant/Testimony.' The Aron Habrit was believed to have held other things, such as Moshes staff and a jar of manna.

MAIN MESSAGE

ADONAI keeps His promises. We may not see them in our lifetime, but we can have confidence that He does keep them. Sometimes it might even be through our children or their children. ADONAI saw that David's heart was good. Because of this, He allowed the Temple to be built to honor David's faithfulness. However, it was not through David that it was built but his son Shlomo.

TRUST   OBEY   LOVE

Haftara 23 (Prophets)

Memory Verse

"Now it was in the heart of David my father to build a house for the name of ADONAI the G-d of Isra'el."
1 Kings 8:17 CJB

Did You Know?

The Ark of the Covenant is still here today. It has been hidden for a long time. Even though some claim to have found it, most people have not yet been allowed to see it.

Promise

1 Kings 8:17-19 CJB

"...Although it was on your heart to build a house for my name, and you did well that it was in your heart, nevertheless you will not build the house. Rather, you will father a son, and it will be he who will build the house for my name."

Shekinah

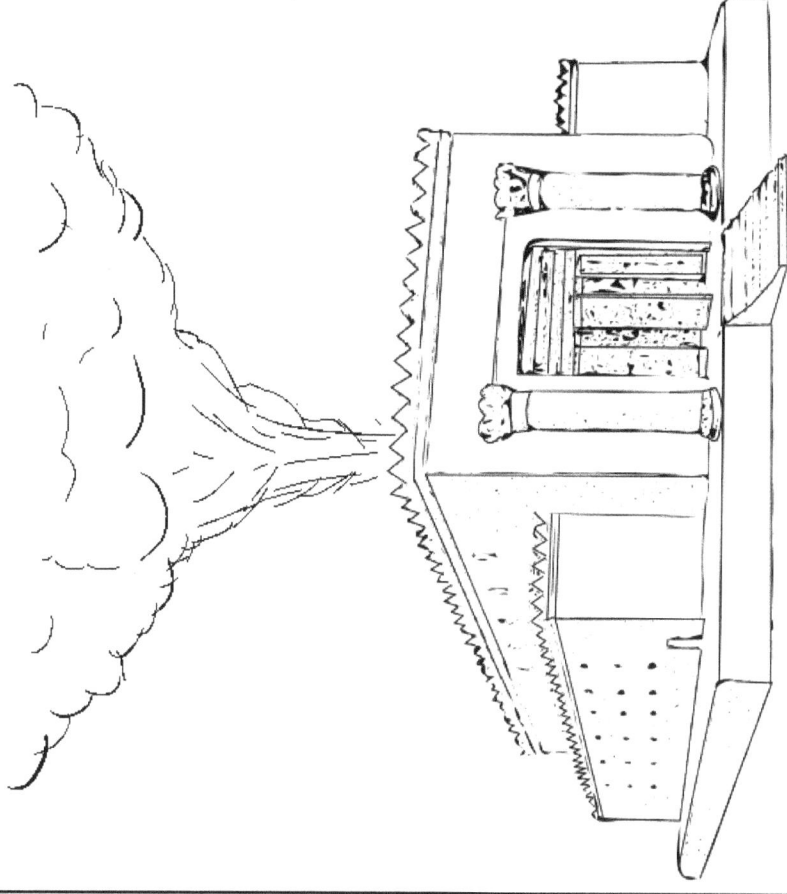

"When the cohanim came out of the Holy Place, the cloud filled the house of ADONAI." 1 Kings 8:10 CJB

Generational Blessing

Some of ADONAI's blessings flow down generations as they did with David and Shlomo (Solomon). Draw a different coloured line between these generations to show the different ways they could be connected.

1. Grandmother, mother, daughter 2. Grandfather, father, son

3. Grandmother, father, daughter 4. Grandfather, father, daughter

5. Grandmother, father, son 6. Grandfather, mother, son

7. Grandmother, Mother, Son 8. Grandfather, mother, daughter

Acts 2:1-47

B'rit Hadashah 23
(Newer Testament)

STORY SUMMARY

Outpouring of the Spirit: All the believers were gathered for the feast of Shavuot (Feast of Weeks). Suddenly the sound of a violent wind filled the house and tongues of fire came on each one of them. They were filled with the Ruach HaKodesh and instantly spoke in different languages. They went out into the city in the power of the Ruach. When they spoke about Yeshua, foreign people understood them in their own language.

WORD FOCUS

Shavuot: 'Weeks.' It also means 'oath.' Shavuot has been long connected with the giving of the Torah and the 'oath' or 'covenant' made at that time. ADONAI also chose this day to give the Ruach HaKodesh as He promised through Yeshua.

MEMORY VERSE

"They were all filled with the Ruach HaKodesh and began to talk in different languages as the spirit enabled them to speak." Acts 2:4 CJB

MAIN MESSAGE

In the same way ADONAI filled the Tabernacle and the Temple with His shekinah, He filled the faithful believers at Shavuot. All three times ADONAI was represented by fire. 1 Corinthians 6:19 says we are now the Temple of the Ruach HaKodesh. As ADONAI led in times past, He leads today, through the power of the Ruach HaKodesh, which lives inside those who love Him. We need to listen carefully because sometimes we get too busy or distracted and don't hear Him.

PROMISE

"But you will receive power when the Ruach HaKodesh has come upon you; you will be my witnesses..." Acts 1:8 CJB

DID YOU KNOW?

There were people from over sixteen different places, with different languages, that all heard the believers speak in their own language.

Acts 2:1-47 Activity Sheet

Gift of Tongues

This is the name of Yeshua in different languages. Can you recognise any of the languages?

Draw a line from the country flag to the language word.

ישוע

ਯੀਸ਼ੁ

イエス

耶稣

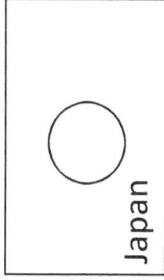
Japan

China

Isra'el

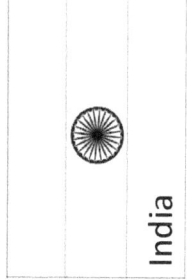
India

Shavuot

"Then they saw what looked like tongues of fire which separated and came to rest on each one of them"

Acts 2:3 CJB

Answers

Parasha 13

Haftara 13

Tzav la-tzav	Line by line
Kav la-kav	A little here, there
Zeir sham	Precept by precept

B'rit Hadashah 13

Parasha 14

Water to blood
Frogs
Lice
Wild beasts
Livestock killed
Infectious sores
Hail Storm

Haftara 14

THAT ALL EGYPT
WILL KNOW I AM
ADONAI

Haftara 15

Don't be afraid,
Ya'akov my
servant;
Don't be
distressed, Isra'el.

B'rit Hadashah 15

Empty
Futile
Vain
Useless
foolish

Parasha 16

When they saw the mighty
deeds ADONAI had done.

B'rit Hadashah 16

B'rit Hadashah 17

Parasha 17

Haftara 17

Across: 2. Peace 3. counsellor 4. Mighty

Down: 1. Everlasting

Parasha 18

Haftara 18

Set the Hebrew
slaves free!

Haftara 19

ADONAI gave Shlomo
wisdom, as he had
promised him; and there
was peace between
Hiram and Shlomo.

1 Kings 5:26.

Parasha 19

Haftara 20

B'rit Hadashah 20

Yeshua is the light of the world

Parasha 21

```
C + + + + + C S + + + L L P L
+ O + + + + U L A + O + U A O
+ + M + + O + U E V + + F R N
+ + + P I + T + I A + + I D G
+ + + C A H L N + + N + C O S
+ + A + O S G U + + + S R N U
+ R + R + + S + F + + + E S F
G + I G N I V I G R O F M S F
+ T + + + + + O + E + + + + E
Y T R U T H F U L N + W + + R
+ + + + + + + + + + A + O + I
+ D N I K + + + + + T + P N +
+ + + + + + + + + + + E + G +
+ + + + + + + + + + + + + + +
+ + + + + + + + + + + + + + +
```

Haftara 21

Reuben, Simeon,
Levi, Judah, Issachar,
Zebulon, Gad, Asher,
Joseph, Benjamin,
Dan, Naphtali

Parasha 22

Remember, shabbat, G-d, Six,
labor, work, seventh, Shabbat,
ADONAI, G-d, work, son, male,
slave, gates, ADONAI, heaven,
everything, blessed, separated.

B'rit Hadashah 22

This is to be a sign between
me and you for all generations." HBBAATS = SHABBAT

B'rit Hadashah 23

Japan
China
Isra'el
India

Parasha 23

Haftara 23

References and websites used

In order of appearance

Yourlivingwater.org

Torah.org

Richard Elofer– weekly Torah study

Creative commons

picscoloring.com

galleryhip.com

Chadbad.org

Wikipedia.org

Freebibleimages.org

Wolfpetrolservices.com

Theclipartwizard.com

Hebrew4christians.com

Shemayisrael.com

Factslides.com

commons.wikimedia.org

Jonkeane.com

Pinterest.com

Flickr.com

Freetheslaves.net

www.ou.org

bereanbiblestudygroup.com

www.unionchapel.org.uk

www.nltblog.com

www.thelostogle.com

www.guernseys.com

www.bibleprophecyupdate.com

ubdavid.org

www.aish.com

www.biblecharts.org

lightofprophecy1844.com

ladylyell.hubpages.com

www.reformjudaism.org

Duncan 1890

www.ingramcontent.com/pod-product-compliance
Lightning Source LLC
LaVergne TN
LVHW081449070426
835508LV00016B/1418